AT THIS POINT

REFLECTIONS OF A HARD-HEADED, IMPERFECT FOLLOWER OF JESUS CHRIST

By James H. Evans

MISSIONAL PRESS
-NASHVILLE, TN-

At This Point: Reflections of a Hard-Headed, Imperfect Follower of Jesus Christ

Copyright © 2023 James H. Evans / BENCHMARK Adventure Ministries

Published by Missional Press, Nashville, TN, a subsidiary of 610Media.
missionalpressbooks.com

All rights reserved. No part of this publication may be reproduced, stored in a retrieval system, or transmitted in any form or by any means—electronic, mechanical, photocopy, recording, or any other means—except for brief quotation in critical reviews, with the prior permission on the publisher.

Unless otherwise indicated, Scripture quotations are from the Holy Bible, New International Version®, NIV®. Copyright © 1973, 1978, 1984, 2011 by Biblica, Inc.® Used by permission of Zondervan. All rights reserved worldwide. www.zondervan.com. The "NIV" and "New International Version" are trademarks registered in the United States Patent and Trademark Office by Biblica, Inc.®

Scripture quotations labeled ESV are from The Holy Bible, English Standard Version®. Copyright © 2001 by Crossway, a publishing ministry of Good News Publishers. Used by permission. All rights reserved.

Scripture quotations labeled MSG are from The Message. Copyright © 1993, 2002, 2018 by Eugene H. Peterson. Used by permission of NavPress. All rights reserved. Represented by Tyndale House Publishers, a Division of Tyndale House Ministries.

Scripture quotations labeled NKJV are from the New King James Version®. Copyright © 1982 by Thomas Nelson. Used by permission. All rights reserved.

Scripture quotations labeled KJV are from the King James Version. Public domain.

ISBN 978-1-7362821-4-4

Cover design: Katie Shull, Shull Design, Nashville, TN.

Printed in the United States of America

AT THIS POINT

Contents

Preface..iv
Acknowledgments..vii
BENCHMARK's R3 Toward Resilience....................1

Part 1

- Introduction...2
1. Responsibility: Where Am I...................................7
2. Responsibility and Blame....................................13
3. Reflection: Introduction 21
4. Reflection: Where I've Been................................29
   Hit by a Truck..36
5. Reflective Connections from My Faith Tradition......43
6. Reflection for Better Teams................................48
7. ReFocus: Foundation..53
8. ReFocus: Practice Leads to Change.....................58
   Mama and Daddy..64
   Reflection Toward a Resilient Life........................74

Part 2

1. I Still Remember...76
2. What Soup Do You Swim In?..............................79
3. Before I ~~Loose~~ Lose My Mind..........................85

i

AT THIS POINT

4. Yet Another Blog………………………………......87
5. Why I Backpack…………………………………….89
6. Steward……………………………………………91
7. The Value of a Known Point……………………94
8. Still in Tension………………………………….. 97
9. Keep Moving or Turn Back...……………………101
10. Immanuel With Us.................................105
11. Post-Christmas Prayer............................108
12. Happy Easter, I Need Jesus....................109
13. No Telling Who I'll Bump Into, 15th Marathon......112
14. Still Learning from Doing, 16th Marathon.............115
15. Best Trail Magic......................................119
16. Layering..123
17. I Remember You......................................127
18. Cannot Be Explained Medically...............130
19. Start Again...132
20. Frustrating People for 25 Years..............135
21. Fifteen Minutes Matter............................138
22. I Broke a Rib...142
23. Worshiping Porcelain..............................145
24. Fast & refocus.......................................146
25. Eleven Minutes......................................149
26. 4x4x48: Toward Birthday Endurance......................151
27. 4x4x48: Toward Physical Resilience........................160
28. 4x4x48: Toward Life Change................................167
29. Things I Don't Like..................................174
30. Be Still or Act..175
31. Gratitude..178
32. Grief...186

AT THIS POINT

Part 3

BENCHMARK History/Foundations……………......189

1. April 17, 1993, An Open Letter……………………191
2. What's a benchmark?……………………………….202
3. Frustrating People for 25 Years,
   March 15, 2018 Dinner Address…………..………204
4. We're OK…………………………………………….210
5. 2022 Ask the Founder—Almost—Anything
   About BENCHMARK……………………………….212
6. These Colors Have Meaning: Red, Black, White……..224

The End: Tell Me "Bye"……………………………230

Endnotes……………………………………………..238
Influential Books……………………………………245

AT THIS POINT

Preface

Though I have spent my life in pursuit of God, I often sense that God lies just around the next bend in the trail, just behind the next tree in the forest. I keep walking because I like where the journey has led me thus far, because other paths seem more problematic than my own, and because I yearn for the resolution of the plot. – Philip Yancey, *Soul Survivor*[1]

And I said, 'Here am I. Send me!' (Isaiah 6:8)

"My name is James. The most important thing you need to know about me is that I am a hard-headed, imperfect follower of Jesus Christ. The second most important thing is that I'm not here to push that down your throat. In polite company, people aren't supposed to talk about four things: politics, religion, sex, or money. But I'll talk about any of those. Now . . . I wouldn't say I was good at all of them, but I will talk about them."

That paragraph serves as my introduction at just about every ministry event I lead with adults, with some modifications when I serve children and teenagers. I do not like to sneak up on people who may not have my worldview, especially after they have signed risk and liability paperwork with BENCHMARK Adventure Ministries at the top.

I have spent my life looking carefully at what is, as well as I could understand it. My sincere desire has been the development

AT THIS POINT

of the people I get to influence. It hasn't been smoothing the ruffled feathers of administrators or leaders whose desires appear to be maintenance.

I have worked well for only a few leaders. I seem to take too much responsibility for the stewardship I have been given. I work at it. It captivates my attention. I take it as a spiritual stewardship, one I often hold too tightly. The leader expects me to invest deeply but to hold it so loosely that their word sways my direction . . . without question.

But I do question. Everything. I question why leaders do what they do. I question their motives. I listen to their words and then watch their actions. If they think I have been difficult on them, they have no idea what I expect of myself.

A dear friend of mine, Sam Johnson, told me in the '90s that people don't like the "Why?" question. He's right. Yet I've spent much of my adult life asking "Why?" and creating for myself all kinds of difficulties. I hear I've created difficulties for others too.

I have taken seriously the words of Christ to make disciples. It is this command that has spurred me on.

I attended a Bible college that was known to train preachers and missionaries. While both of these, and many other methods of ministry, are admirable, I didn't think I was being led into either. On many occasions, I honestly presented myself to God asking where He was leading me and if either of these vocational pursuits were to become mine.

My friend, Kevin Lauthern, knew I was searching and suggested I take a Christian education course. Sitting in that college class the first time, I wondered if this would be the class I'd get a better idea of the direction I should be pointed in.

AT THIS POINT

A young, bright teacher named Jonathan Thigpen taught "Organization and Administration of Christian Education" in 1981. It was his first-year teaching, but he spoke with a knowledge and practicality that I benefited from. At that college, Christian education was the study of all local church-based ministry except the pulpit ministry. I was hopeful.

Thanks for the recommendation, Kevin.

I was sitting about midway back in the classroom as Mr. Thigpen taught about the instruction of 2 Timothy 2:2. The King James Version of the Bible still rattles around in my head today: "And the things that thou hast heard of me among many witnesses, the same commit thou to faithful men, who shall be able to teach others also." The New International Version translates commit as entrust, and faithful as reliable. Both the ideas "commit to be faithful" and "entrust to be reliable" lead to the idea of stewardship.

I wanted to be faithful. I didn't know what I should do as a vocation, but in that class, at that moment, I committed to being a faithful man. I wanted to be a man who could be entrusted with something of great value and would steward it well.

Have I always been sure that I was on the right path, actively being a steward of what God has given me? Mostly.

Sometimes.

Near the end of the last semester of my senior year in Bible College, I was given the opportunity to give testimony standing in front of classmates, teachers, and administration. What I said then, what I knew then, and what I still know now is that when I am done with this life, I only want to hear God say, "Well done, good and faithful servant."

Yes, here I am . . . at this point.

AT THIS POINT

Acknowledgments

We hear people who call themselves "self-made" or some other personally focused declaration. They "pulled themselves up by their bootstraps," so to speak. And while it is true that people wouldn't be where they are without their own effort, it is short sighted to think they have gotten wherever they are solely on their own.

We are all influenced by our past: the people who brought us into the world, hired us for our first job, taught us helpful lessons, and by those who have hindered or hurt us.

I still remember my first-grade teacher, Mrs. Eason, who started my adjustment to school; Mrs. Dart influencing me in regular classes from fifth grade all the way through high school; and Mr. Robertson teaching me how to build stuff in woodshop and how to be exacting in drafting class.

Billy Price, through our entire Wayne County education, was my first best friend from elementary school playground swings through high school graduation.

Wayne Duncan was Scoutmaster for most of my time in Boy Scouts. He could look at a block of wood and see a detailed bird. When he was done carving and painting, that's exactly what it looked like. I think he did the same for me. He encouraged me to lead, making me a junior assistant Scoutmaster after I earned Eagle.

AT THIS POINT

The men and women of the First Free Will Baptist Church in Jesup, Georgia, where I first chose to follow Jesus Christ and where I learned to worship, financially helped me go to college. Mrs. Brannen hired me for the summer after my freshman year to work in her coat factory, and then I cleaned the warehouse twice a week. She loved me like her own before she hired me and after I worked for her. I can still remember her gentle spirit and smile.

Lehman and Barbara Ward were small business owners, and Mr. Lehman gave me my first paying after-school job.

I could give numerous other examples. Most of the ones who shaped me are slowly leaving this life and moving into the next. Their well-lived lives still influence me in profound and simple ways that I can't fully parse out.

There are unkind and hurtful people who intentionally or unintentionally gave me an example of who I do not want to be or become. I expect I've been that person for others too.

I am especially grateful for:

– Barbara, my wife and mother of our children, who gives me the freedom to be who I am in Christ, allowing me to flourish in the outdoors while showing me more love than I could ever deserve and tolerating more than she should. I decided to marry the first woman who thought she could live with me. And you have. I still love you.

– our children, on whom we practiced parenting, and still are. They have brought more heartbreak than I thought I could bear and more joy than I thought was humanly possible. I am proud of who you are and hopeful of who you will become. I hope this volume will help you to understand your dad.

– John and DeWees Evans, Mama and Daddy, who fed, clothed, and taught me a life of faith in Christ, leaving a lasting

AT THIS POINT

legacy of looking out for others with family as a priority. They taught and modeled a simple life that still positively shapes my life today. I miss you both.

– John Bridger Evans Jr. (Joby) my brother, for reminding me of stories of our admirable parents.

– Sam and Jane Johnson, pioneers in Christian camping in the United States and internationally creators of hands-on leadership development through practical work and biblical discipleship. Your entrepreneurial spirit, hard-working service for Jesus Christ, and an entire life of service to others spurs me on. You have always wanted what was best for me. I am profoundly humbled that you pray for me every day.

– Kinley Winchester whose steady friendship, listening ear, and smart humor, for half my life, have encouraged my abilities. He has spoken just the right word so many times. We have taught, served, and dreamed together. When others have left, you have not. Without your influence, it's likely that BENCHMARK wouldn't continue today or if I'd still be walking the planet.

– Jay Tobin, former Wilderness Leadership Practicum student. Your innovative leadership skillfully navigated military hurdles and persuaded others that caring for Soldiers from an adjusted ministry model would be beneficial. I'm forever thankful that we led the first three BENCHMARK ministry event serving Soldiers by partnering with you, a U.S. Army Chaplain. You have changed my life more than you'll ever know.

– Jonathan Thigpen, my college major professor, captivating educator and preacher, leader of excellence, and early adopter of Macintosh computers. The life you lived was too short. You finished strong with resilience, personal courage, and an abiding faith in Christ leaving so many, including me, permanently better.

AT THIS POINT

– Dr. David Klopfenstein, who deepened my understanding of organizational leadership and instruction, trusting me with his graduate school classroom even while I was his student, and gave me space to lead in settings likely before I thought I was ready.

– Ken Kalisch who with firm kindness and abundant grace allowed me to practice leadership and instruction in a wilderness context all through the 1990s. You were my program manager and teacher, who became my friend. With your wife Fran you have modeled a Christ-focused, principled life of cheerful service; quiet, steady leadership; and a willingness to do what needed to be done to serve others well. It's not an overstatement to say that you have influenced every page of this volume.

– Erik Alfsen led the way during the fourth Chaplains Partnership Initiative (CPI) ministry event with high competence and leadership. I've learned so much about the military context and Soldier ministry from you since 2012. I'll keep telling stories.

– Dana Krull as we developed the fifth and sixth CPI ministry events, increasing my understanding of serving with Chaplains. You've spoken at our ministry celebrations and I am so very thankful. Beginning two years ago, your early editorial expertise brought focus to this manuscript, its theme, and content.

– Henry and Catherine DePhillips read the entire manuscript, asked great questions, affirmed that it sounded like me, and that I had something to say.

– Anna Poole heard about this writing project while my wife, Barbara, and I hiked a mere 60 miles during her 2,193.1 mile, 2021 Appalachian Trail thru hike. Anna recently made time to read much of it adding valuable improvements.

– Jonathan Turnbough and Joshua Eidson read early attempts and more recent writings reassuring me to continue.

AT THIS POINT

– Tracy Phillips also read it with attention to the reader. Your opinion matters.

– Kurt Boucher is one of the finest U.S. Army Religious Affairs NCOs I have had the pleasure to serve with. You reminded me of ideas I needed to include and some I needed to say better. This work is better because of you. May God bless your next chapter.

– Carol Reid completely read and edited this manuscript twice offering immeasurable guidance. Your generous gift of time and editorial skill is kindness I do not deserve. While refining this project to make it better, I can still hear you saying with great freedom, "It's your book."

– Chelsea and Stuart, the staff of BENCHMARK Adventure Ministries, who have likely heard too much about this near-eternal process of getting these ideas out of my head and into pixels.

– BENCHMARK Board of Directors who years ago encouraged me to write more, sharing BENCHMARK stories and instructional content.

The list of real, personal influencers is far too long to list here. I'm thankful for those whose ideas and relationships have been integrated from a variety of personal, academic, professional, and religious influences. There is no attempt to take credit for every idea as my original idea.

AT THIS POINT

BENCHMARK'S R3 Toward Resilience
Part 1

This instructional content shapes every ministry event that BENCHMARK Adventure Ministries leads. Before they shaped anything else, these ideas first shaped me.

BENCHMARK's R3 Toward Resilience

R3 toward Resilience is Responsibility/Reflection/Refocus, a present/past/future framework, influenced by the integration of philosophy, sociology, theology, psychology, my faith tradition, and abundant personal mistakes with guidance from and the examples of others. It is not a specific series of lectures, classes or discussion questions. It is a process that's helpful to move toward a healthier, happier life more focused on the end and a better life before that end.

AT THIS POINT

Introduction
BENCHMARK's R3 Toward Resilience

Have you ever been at the end of it? Your wit's end? Your rope? Your patience?

Have you ever gotten to the point where you thought you didn't have what it takes to meet the demands of life? That you couldn't take on whatever was next?

Or have things been going pretty well for you but something seems off, your responses seem out of sync with your reality?

I have.

None of us will get through this life unscathed, unhurt, without trouble or suffering. No one. We'll either do it to ourselves, someone will do it to us, or it will come on its own.

If you have come to that point, then you've waded right into life or it's run you down. That moment of doubt when you are uncertain is part of what makes you human. Actually, it's what makes you, potentially, real.

You don't have to stay there, but how long you stay matters.

Resilience is a growing theme in our culture, and for good reason. Resilience is countercultural, running against the zeitgeist.

We chase equilibrium. We don't like change. The potential for personal growth and maturity declines dramatically if we value its pursuit too highly.

AT THIS POINT

While others have done admirable work into resilience, BENCHMARK needed to explore it from our own adventure-oriented, follower of Jesus Christ, leadership development, and spiritual formation perspective. How can we dig into resilience from the viewpoint of significant life-change?

Resilience is character working itself out in daily life. It's perseverance, stick-to-itiveness, staying power. It's the ability to take a hit, learn from it, adjust, and then get back at it. It's developing, over time, mental, emotional, spiritual, and physical depth and drawing from that depth to weather the storms of life.

I've found that pliability and elasticity are helpful synonyms to keep in mind. A retired Marine friend says "Semper Gumby," or "Always Flexible." While being flexible can be admirable, being too pliable can lead us not to hold enough form to be reliable. We can simply take the shape of whatever situation we are in. Sometimes we shouldn't go with the flow.

Resilience isn't forged in rigidity either. If our character and responses are too rigid, we'll crack or crack others. There is a practical tension between pliability and rigidity. We can be too rigid or too fluid. Neither will serve us well or help us serve others well.

Character and values should shape our choices, and trust is foundational for all healthy relationships. Trust can be built, damaged, or destroyed. When people can believe what you say and know you will follow through on what you have said you will do, trust increases, relationships deepen.

Decisions based on high values with high character will move us toward resilience.

The R3 toward Resilience instructional framework was developed though our partnership with U.S. Army Unit Ministry

AT THIS POINT

Teams through our groundbreaking Chaplains Partnership Initiative serving Chaplains, their Religious Affairs Specialists, and the Soldiers and Families they serve.

The U.S. Army takes resilience seriously. Its Master Resilience Training is a ten-day training program designed to "produce junior leaders with the capability to teach proven resilience skills to the Soldiers in their teams, squads, and platoons in order to enhance their performance and increase their resiliency, both individually and collectively."[1] Although I haven't been through the course myself, I have heard Soldiers describe some of what they have received as resilience training at the unit level. They call it "death by PowerPoint." That's not the direction I want to go in.

Though our Chaplains Partnership Initiative ministry events are developed in partnership with a Chaplain, not every aspect of the retreat is specifically faith based. A Chaplain's role is to provide religious support to every Soldier, regardless of their faith tradition.

According to the U.S. Army, the Chaplain's mission is to bring Soldiers to God and God to Soldiers. The Chaplain's Creed[2] also includes the affirmation: "I will never disrespect another's faith group." Soldiers and Family Members who participate in Chaplain-led retreats are free to opt out of any faith-focused session. I've noticed that some opt out even while their body is present.

Human beings live out our values, both the ones we state and the ones we don't. It's a consistent notion found in practical philosophy, social psychology, and theology. It's certainly consistent with the teaching of the Holy Bible and the life of Jesus Christ.

AT THIS POINT

The question that nags me is this: How can BENCHMARK develop teaching content that connects to our action/reflection model of doing adventure, making it true to who we are as a faith-based ministry in line with the character of God and a relationship with Jesus Christ, with application to daily life without it being a Bible study or presented as a "sermon?"

Challenge accepted.

My days at Wheaton Graduate School were soaked in praxis which encouraged thoughtful reflection on the past in order to understand the present. Through this process, decisions–hopefully wise ones–will be made for the future. Weekly, just for one class, we read a book and wrote a three-page theory/practice integration paper. It was an attempt to pull together theoretical concepts and theological ideas to significantly affect practice.

In other words, what is a meaningful idea and then how do I apply it to daily life? I'm indebted to Dr. David Klopfenstein, aka Klop, who detailed an idea of Aristotle praxis that still sticks with me. More simply put:

Praxis is looking back on the past in order to make sense of the present for the purpose of future, wise decision-making.

For BENCHMARK, praxis shapes our integrated R3 toward Resilience process drawing from a variety of personal, academic, professional, and religious influences for the purpose of life change.

The concepts behind what would become BENCHMARK's R3 toward Resilience were being shaped in my head and heart over thirty years ago. That's confident testimony that I picked up maybe

AT THIS POINT

a third of what Drs. Klop, Jim Plueddemann, Dwayne Elmer, and Gene Gibbs were trying to teach just on the educational ministries side of the school.

And before that, these ideas were being shaped while in college, and in the piney woods of south Georgia by my parents, Sunday school teachers, church leaders, visiting missionaries, public school teachers, Scout leaders, little league coaches, neighbors and employers.

It is from these varying influences that BENCHMARK's R3 toward Resilience has developed.

The idea for BENCHMARK and the hope for those we serve is to lay out an adventure and relational framework presented by candid and honest leadership to get participants to consider how they currently live, what from their past affects the way they currently live, and how they want to live in the future. We're trying to get at that head and heart connection, now, to affect their future.

The hope is that these simple ideas, firmly influenced by my faith tradition, will help people live a healthier life and be more resilient.

AT THIS POINT

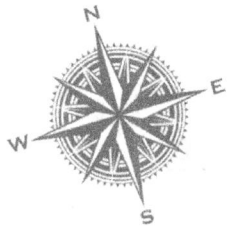

Chapter 1
Responsibility: Where am I?

If you don't have a goal, any road will get you there.
– Yogi Berra

But he knows the way that I take; when he has tested me, I will come forth as gold. (Job 23:10)

BENCHMARK's R3 Toward Resilience

BENCHMARK's R3 toward Resilience has become the framework on which other ministry event themes can hang and be developed. Three words provide the structure for that framework; Responsibility, Reflection, and Refocus.

Each of these three key words begin with "re" which comes from Latin, meaning "again and again." This indicates repetition. We should bump into these core points of contact repeatedly.

Resilience begins with having an idea of where you are.

AT THIS POINT

Where am I?

I've been asking myself that question for a long time. It's a haunting, critical question that surfaces for just about every person in one way or another.

You have to start where you are, not where you're not.

I remember asking it of myself in May of 1990. I was a student on a graduate level, sixteen-day wilderness trip. This leadership development and spiritual growth experience was staged in the great outdoors of northern Wisconsin and the Upper Peninsula of Michigan. Two full weeks of sleeping on the ground under a clear plastic tarp, cooking food on wood fires, and using backpacking, canoeing, route finding, and bushwhacking to test our personal mettle while exploring our relationship with God.

It can be chilly for a Southern boy up that way in May.

Map and compass work reminded me of my teenage orienteering attempts in Boy Scouts. Now as an adult, my wilderness instructor would ask, "Do you know where you are? Would you show me on the map?" Sometimes I had no idea where in the woods I was. Other times I kind of had an idea where in the woods I was. Sometimes others in my group had ideas but we needed to have a better idea. We'd work on it together sometimes and alone sometimes.

You don't figure out where you are until you learn some skills to learn where you are. So, I tried to learn.

The Wilderness Learning Seminar was part of the High Road program with Honey Rock, the Northwoods campus of Wheaton College led by Ken Kalisch. It stretched me as a follower of Jesus Christ, training me to know Him more deeply and to lead more effectively. The foundation was laid before the trip with Bible

AT THIS POINT

studies tracing God's use of the wilderness as a place of growth and training. It continued with reading and discussing three classic thin volumes: Man's Search for Meaning, Your God is Too Small, and The Mark of a Christian. All three remain on my bookshelf to this day.

By 1990, I had earned an undergraduate degree in Bible and Christian Education and a Master's degree in Educational Ministries. I had been married for almost two years. I had some training, education, and experience. But this particular training experience was coming, apparently, at just the right time. It was good, and hard, and personal.

In June of that same summer I began training to be a wilderness instructor with High Road. The intensity increased on all fronts. I needed to know how to read a map and use a compass not only for myself but for the students I would lead as a High Road instructor. I needed to be able to find my location in order to keep the students on track and in case something went wrong. I also needed to have a better understanding of who I was as a person, a follower of Christ, a leader: why I made the decisions I made, how my emotions affected my decisions, and how my past affected where I was.

That summer I started leading longer wilderness trips, first with some middle schoolers and then in August with entering college freshman and transfer students. Later I led trips with other adults. Ken allowed me to get in the woods as a High Road instructor all through the '90s leading sixteen wilderness trips, each lasting sixteen to nineteen days.

On those trips, I'd regularly ask my students, "Would you show me on the map where you think you are?" When they weren't sure, I'd tell them to go ask their group and come back.

AT THIS POINT

Other times, I'd ask more pointedly, "Do you have any idea where you are?"

In 1993, the simple question, "Where am I?" influenced the naming of the nonprofit ministry I lead. BENCHMARK Adventure Ministries isn't called benchmark because we think this ministry is the standard by which all others should be measured. That's a common usage of the word these days. Our name is taken from a tiny topographic map symbol, a benchmark. It's most often an equilateral triangle with a small mark in the center. When you find one in the wild, that symbol is etched into a bronze or aluminum disc set in stone.

A benchmark has two planes: vertical and horizontal. In this country, the United States Geological Survey (USGS) determines the location of each specific benchmark and its relationships to other features like roads, streams, or mountains. That's the horizontal plane. Vertically, the USGA confirms its elevation in relation to sea level.

Whether in the wilderness or in the city, a benchmark is a known, permanent point of reference that can help us better understand exactly where we are, almost anywhere in the world.

The personal assessment implications of that simple symbol to human relationships are significant. BENCHMARK designs interactive adventures to help individuals assess their horizontal relationship with other people, their surroundings, and Creation, and their vertical relationship with God. The small mark in the middle of the triangle symbolizes the high value of a Christ-centered, Biblical worldview and how that emphasis affects the whole person. The three sides of the triangle represent BENCHMARK's focus on the whole person: the mind, the heart, and the will. A BENCHMARK experience helps you to better

AT THIS POINT

understand where you are and will challenge you to evaluate the way you think, feel, and act in light of biblical principles.

We're BENCHMARK because I want to be reminded regularly that I need to assess where I am at a known point, today, this moment. I regularly need to honestly assess. I need to know where I am — or at least where I think I am.

Self-Check

Over the years, "Where am I?" has added layers and depth to my own thinking. It's not just about where I am physically, though that is a good thing to know. It applies to other aspects of life: emotionally, intellectually, socially, spiritually, and vocationally. Knowing where I am physically can often be a path to exploring "where am I" in the other five areas.

I've benefited from the compact and content-rich Building Blocks for Longer Life and Ministry[1] of Dr. Tommy Yessick's development of six wellness dimensions. His "Assessment of Total Well-Being" has provided me with valuable insight based on my own responses to seventy-eight Likert scale questions with almost always, often, about half the time, occasionally, or rarely. I've taken this assessment at least four times.

After gaining a better understanding of how my emotions affect my actions and attitudes, it has been helpful to see the effect six emotions have on the six wellness dimensions. I've merged these compatible ideas into BENCHMARK's R3 6x6 self-check.

This simple 6x6 self-check can be a pre- and post-event evaluation tool to simply record "where you are."

AT THIS POINT

Start with where you are in the present, now. Are you glad, sad, mad, hurt, afraid, ashamed? Which of these emotional touchpoints would you choose to describe where you are in each of the wellness dimensions of physical, emotional, intellectual, social, spiritual, vocational?

Would you take 3 minutes to make notes on the R3 6x6 self-check?

Being a resilient person starts with where am I.

BENCHMARK's R3 6x6 self-check

BENCHMARK's R3 for Resilience	physical	emotional	intellectual	social	spiritual	vocational
glad						
sad						
mad						
hurt						
afraid						
ashamed						

AT THIS POINT

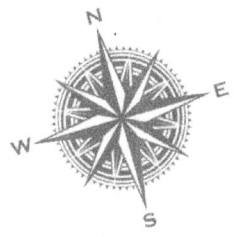

Chapter 2
RESPONSIBILITY AND BLAME

Success is another form of failure if we lose sight of our priorities.
– Joe Rodgers (former Ambassador to France)

You can't wait until life isn't hard anymore before you decide to be happy. - Jane "Nightbirde" Marczweski

For most of us on the planet, we move from one thing to the next without giving much thought to where we've been, where we're going, or what place God has in any of it. This lack of personal introspection may even be a high American value.

Figuring out where you are is an important endeavor. If you don't know where you are, it will be difficult to figure out where you need to go. 'Where I am?' is asking about now, the present.

You don't have to be where others are. It's not one size fits all. You may be in a great spot. Celebrate. Or maybe you're not. It's an honest check-in. You don't have to be in a good place, but you may be. Either way, for now, it's OK.

AT THIS POINT

Thirty years ago my wife and I participated in a workshop led by Dr. Chris Thurman based on his book The Lies We Believe[1]. I've gone back to Dr. Thurman's teaching periodically, and recently while listening to the thirtieth anniversary presentation, he helped me to find the word I was searching for — "true." In determining where I am, it just has to be true. It's not about where you would like to be but where you really are.

You might not be in a good spot. You might be lost or at least not know where you are at the moment. Be honest about that. Look at it square in the eye and determine what is true.

So where are you? Can you slow your heart and mind down enough to get the best assessment you can, now?

Wherever you are, you need to own it.

Responsibility

All of my relationships are better when I progressively, more and more, take responsibility for my actions and attitude. All.

It is most beneficial with my significant, intimate relationships; my wife, our kids, my close friends, work associates, and ministry event participants. As a human being I have the capacity to manage my actions and attitude.

Emotions just are. Here they come. There are times when I am angry and I can't tell you why that is, at that moment. I just am. At times, grief creeps in for no apparent reason. But there it is. When beauty overwhelms me, and I am glad, I should enjoy it.

Emotions feed actions and attitudes. We live in a culture where emotions are used to justify whatever we do and however we act. Yet, we do not have to be ruled by our emotions.

Whenever emotions surface, what we do next matters.

AT THIS POINT

Soldier participants in our Chaplains Partnership Initiative ministry events has some awareness of The Army Values.[2] When we are exploring this critical point of Responsibility, I'll ask them which Army Value needs to be engaged in order to take Responsibility. Someone will undoubtedly shout out "Personal Courage."

I'll ask "Why is that?" The comments by participants are insightful. It takes courage to look yourself in the eye. It takes courage to see your actions honestly. It takes courage to firmly say, "This is where I am."

Taking responsibility for my actions and attitude does take personal courage. It's a willingness to take a clear, accurate look at where you are.

In the first century, Saul of Tarsus was a threat to the early Church of Jesus Christ. He was its persecutor. In time, he became a follower and missionary, had a name change to Paul, and later was a prisoner in Rome because he followed Jesus. While in prison, he wrote letters to the churches he helped to begin. In his letter to the Church at Ephesus, Paul writes, "As a prisoner for the Lord, then, I urge you to live a life worthy of the calling you have received. Be completely humble and gentle; be patient, bearing with one another in love" (Ephesians 4:1, 2).

Humble is a word we don't hear much. It doesn't often describe politicians, business leaders, or frankly, church leadership. It doesn't often describe most of the rest of us either.

In *Be Rich*, a study of the letter to the church at Ephesus, Warren Wiersbe writes that humility "means knowing ourselves, accepting ourselves, and being ourselves to the glory of God. God does not condemn you when you accept yourself and your gifts (Romans 12:3). He just does not want us to think more highly of

AT THIS POINT

ourselves than we ought to—or less highly than we ought to."[3] From Romans 12:3 we learn that we are to have "sober judgment"; a clear minded, honest assessment of who we really are.

Responsibility has a dual effect; it's good for us and it's good for others, too. It is supported by this challenge to another church that Paul started. "Do nothing out of selfish ambition or vain conceit. Rather, in humility value others above yourselves, not looking to your own interests but each of you to the interests of the others" (Philippians 2:3-4).

Please read that last sentence again.

We move toward Responsibility when we look out for our own interests. We're not only supposed to look to our own interests, we are to humbly "value others above ourselves," and look to the interests of others. We are to act in others' best interest.

Acting in others' best interest is love. This attention to others is not a fluid, what-ever-you-do-is-all-right-with-me, "nice" idea of love. It's the concept of love that genuinely, above all else, wants what is best for someone else, short-term, long-term, and eternally.

My most significant relationships are better when I take responsibility for where I am today. The point is, figure out where you are.

If you are having trouble figuring it out, you may need to reach out to a truth-telling friend or a professional: counselor, therapist, pastor.

We move toward responsibility when we are courageous. We move toward responsibility when we determine what is true. We move toward responsibility when we do so in humility. We move

AT THIS POINT

toward responsibility when we act in our own best interest. We move toward responsibility when we act in others' best interest.

Responsibility is well-supported when we are courageous, when we practice humility and when we act in others' best interest.

So what are you thinking about now? Jot down what you're thinking about now in the margin.

Blame

Stephen Covey writes, "Look at the word responsibility—"response-ability"—the ability to choose your response. Highly proactive people recognize that responsibility. They do not blame circumstances, conditions, or conditioning for their behavior. Their behavior is a product of their own conscious choice, based on values, rather than a product of their conditions, based on feeling."[3]

We all need to step toward our own responsibility saying, "This is on me. I 'take' it." Blame says, "This is on you. I 'deflect' it."

Blame has serious implications for our personal interactions or work relationships. Blame, in fact, has become a national American pastime. It's always someone else's fault.

In the Genesis account of creation, Jehovah God created the world and everything in it, including man, and later woman. Humans had a perfect relationship with God. There were rules. "And the LORD God commanded the man, "You are free to eat from any tree in the garden; but you must not eat from the tree of the knowledge of good and evil, for when you eat from it you will certainly die" (Genesis 2:16, 17).

The woman was tempted by the crafty serpent. "When the woman saw that the fruit of the tree was good for food and

AT THIS POINT

pleasing to the eye, and also desirable for gaining wisdom, she took some and ate it. She also gave some to her husband, who was with her, and he ate it" (Genesis 3:6).

Both the woman and the man made a choice. They chose to disobey. That disobedience damaged the perfect relationship they had with God and put all of humanity into a world of hurt.

And then there it is, that question, "Where are you?" (Genesis 3:9). God knew where they were. The man and the woman heard the sound of the Lord God as he was walking in the garden in the cool of the day, and they hid. They felt shame.

The man's initial response? Blame. He said, "The woman you put here with me—she gave me some fruit from the tree, and I ate it" (Genesis 3:12). The man, later called Adam, led the way for the rest of us. He blamed God who gave him the woman, later called Eve.

Blaming God for my response to a situation is gutsy—and very foolish.

Eve, the woman, made a choice. Adam, the man, made a choice. Since creation, humans have blamed each other and God for their own choices and responses. And so it continues.

Clerow Wilson Jr. was a twentieth-century American comedian and actor best known for the Flip Wilson Show in the late '60s and early '70s. I remember him saying "The devil made me do it." For a comedic line, it was pretty funny. For the practical reality of good human relationships, it's blame. It's someone else's fault; I'm not responsible.

I've heard people say more than a few times, "You made me mad." Apparently, I have that effect on some people.

I likely had something to do with their response. I may have set the stage for it. I may have done something that I shouldn't have

AT THIS POINT

done. But, I made you do it? If I made you, then I control you, and I don't want to control you.

Each of us needs to take responsibility for our own actions. I am not in control of your responses. I will not take responsibility for your actions, attitudes, or emotions, nor should you take responsibility for mine.

Your response to my actions and attitude may even be very justified and reasonable, but your response is still yours. I can easily convince myself to justify my actions and response because of what the other person did.

Too many click-bait worthy news headlines have some form of the words "bash" or "slam." News headlines justify being mean spirited and snarky because they are trying to grab our attention. I'm trying to avoid those headlines because it draws me into being who I do not want to be.

As a person who desires to grow in admirable character, the ability to respond should move me to responsibility for my actions, attitude, and the emotions that affect them. But, sometimes, I hide. Hear me well: I am often not quick to take responsibility for actions and attitude. I am slower to it. I often need some time to roll it around in my mind, to rethink what happened, what I said or did and how I responded. I need to be convinced of what I did or said before I can own it. And I may not want to own it. I may need to own it.

If my tendency is to more slowly take responsibility for my actions, then I'm sure not going to take responsibility for something I did not do. I'm not going to say I'm sorry just to smooth it over.

Admirable character is built like a bunker, one sandbag at a time. We can build, little by little, one choice at a time, to take a

AT THIS POINT

step toward admirable character as we learn to be responsible for our own actions. It takes personal courage and integrity to do it.

Responsibility and blame are connected, but not in a productive way. We all have to fight the tide of blame. We all need to progressively, more and more, take responsibility for our actions and our attitudes. As I see it, you have three choices: I will, I won't, or I might.

Would this be a good time to remind you that BENCHMARK's R3 6x6 self-check may be helpful to you in exploring this idea?

AT THIS POINT

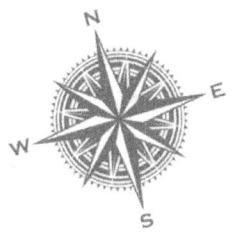

Chapter 3
Reflection Introduction

The unexamined life is not worth living. – Socrates

On Family: You spend 17 or 18 years of your life living with these people and the rest of your life working it out. – Margaret Smith, comedian

I'm captivated by the Appalachian Trail (AT).

When I was a kid my family vacationed a few times in the north Georgia mountains and the Great Smoky Mountains National Park. I hiked some miles on the AT. Hiking the whole trail that runs from my home state of Georgia to Maine seemed like a dream too big for a kid to consider.

As an adult, I regained interest in backpacking with long and short mileage days. At the insistence of my fiancé in 1988, I planned a three-day, two-night backpacking trip in the Great Smoky Mountains National Park as a part of our honeymoon. We

AT THIS POINT

hiked a short section of the AT and trails connecting to Mount LeConte.

Yes, we're still married.

I don't know how many miles we have hiked and backpacked together since.

I've long thought that I, or maybe we, might do a thru-hike completing the entire 2,198.4-mile AT in a single hiking season. If I didn't really like my work, that may have risen in priority. Most hikers plan about six months to thru hike the entire trail.

In October of 1995 I planned the first "Backpack for BENCHMARK" — 71.7 miles on the AT in 72 hours in the Great Smoky Mountains National Park from Fontana Dam to Davenport Gap. You know, a walk-a-thon with a backpack to raise much needed operating funds. Mark, an original Advisory Board member, wrote a support letter on behalf of BENCHMARK and called it a "daring exploit." But Hurricane Opal tore up the Smokies that year so I opted for 68.1 miles between Pickett State Park, Tennessee, and Cumberland Falls State Park, Kentucky, on the Sheltowee Trace by myself. Donors gave $1012.40.

The next year, I hiked 73.6 miles on the AT in 72 hours from one end of the Great Smoky Mountain National Park, Fontana Dam to I-40. I took 150 pictures on that trip because I was by myself and wanted to share it with others when I was done. I still have very fond memories of that solo trip. I learned that I didn't really want to hike that hard again by myself.

It's that affinity for the AT that led BENCHMARK to begin our Appalachian Trail Outreach, sharing our lives in Christ through simple service, prayer, and good food in an unexpected location. Since 2008 we have greeted hundreds of hikers in north Georgia

AT THIS POINT

with "Would you like an apple?" Periodically we'll ask if we can pray with or for them.

We also do a Gear Shake Down to help hikers reduce their pack weight. There are three rules.

Rule 1 - This is your stuff. You brought it here and you can leave with it all.

Rule 2 - Pull out everything you want me to see. I'll tell you what I think about what you've packed. Consider how much you can put on all at once. Remember: everything weighs something.

Rule 3 - Refer to Rule #1. This is your stuff. You brought it here and you can leave with it all.

When interacting with AT thru-hikers, it's not unusual to be asked "Do you have a trail name?"

Trail names are a curious tradition and an intricate part of the long-distance hiking culture. Most often you earn a trail name after you've done something or experienced something, and the name is typically given to you by someone else.

In some ways trail names are part of a rite of passage for hikers. They span the range of the sublime to the ridiculous, from silly to profane. You abandon your former name, your former life, and take on a new name for this new journey.

In 2011, BENCHMARK partnered with Cincinnati Christian Schools to plan a spring Wilderness Journey specifically for their Enrichment, Service, and Ministry Week. We designed a seven-day adventure utilizing backpacking and wilderness skills in the mountains of western North Carolina along the Appalachian Trail. The fitting theme was Leadership - Learn it, Practice it, Mentored in it.

Seventeen students were divided into three smaller travel groups which consisted of students plus school leadership and a

AT THIS POINT

BENCHMARK instructor. Priscilla and Mark led three males and three females for a group total of eight. David and Sarah led two males and five females. Their group totaled nine.

Kim and I led a group of three females in their last semester of their high school senior year. For the second time in my trip-leading adventures, it would be James and just women. They were all bright and thoughtful, very positive examples of good parenting and an admirable educational experience. These girls came ready for an adventure and willing to learn.

When you're hiking and living just about every hour of every day together for a week, all kinds of conversations come up: fun, silly, insightful, historical, serious, biblical, philosophical, and practical. And since we're on the Appalachian Trail, everyone needs a trail name. Each of these names took shape out of our shared experiences, and for us, each person had to approve of their trail name.

Natalie, trail name: Mudd. It was a popular brand of fashionable clothing. On the trip, Natalie also found plenty of trail mud formed from the springtime rains. Or maybe the mud found her.

Lindsey, trail name: Snail. She was a runner. Fast. She did everything fast and well. So, if you're fast, your name has to be the not-so-fast forest creature we saw on the trail.

Melissa, trail name: Karaoke, also TMI (Too Much Information). This girl could sing and she sang all the time with quite a repertoire. She also periodically told us entirely too much of what we weren't sure we needed to know.

Kim, an admired teacher whose trail name became Trillium. This spring flower's simple beauty was evident along the trail with alternating threes of leaves and petals which reminds me of the

AT THIS POINT

common symbols of the Trinity. We all liked the flower and the group thought the name fit her well.

Mine was Rafiki with obvious connections to the 1994 Disney classic, The Lion King. I couldn't get over being linked to a witchdoctor, and a baboon at that. I was pretty sure my backside wasn't colorful.

But Rafiki does give me reason to pause. Maybe you remember in the movie. It's right after Simba sees his father in a "very peculiar" cosmic display in the night sky, and considers going back to his home. Simba ponders the difficulties of going back. Rafiki reminds Simba that he can "either run from it, or . . . learn from it."

Did you catch that pretty good advice from a witchdoctor baboon from a popular movie. The choice is run or learn. Perhaps I shouldn't have resisted the trail names chosen by those four women.

Looking Back

Why do I need to look back on the past? Well, just like a trail name, it takes our mind back to a past event and the circumstances. Just a word, a smell, a touch or a taste can bring a flood of memories back. Sometimes it sparks joy, other times grief.

Several of the Chaplains Partnership Initiative (CPI) ministry events have had only male, unmarried Soldier participants. They are strong, bright, and young. BENCHMARK had not been serving Soldiers long and Chaplain (CPT) Dana Michael Krull became an early adopter helping to shape our approach to ministry with Soldiers. Dana, now honorably discharged, was a former infantry

AT THIS POINT

officer and later Battalion Chaplain with the 4th Ranger Training Battalion and then the 3rd Battalion, 75th Ranger Regiment.

Dana cut through the military status quo and helped create space with Chaplains for ministry a little out of the normal. Dana and I began exploring the theme that's since developed into a BENCHMARK staple. We wanted to get at ideas that are at the core of each Soldier's being in order to help them question what they may not have questioned before.

When you get to serve a group of Soldiers who are some of the most mentally and physically strong, brightest young men in military service, of course you should get them to explore the question: "What does it mean to be a man?" which guides pointed, helpful discussions, and interactions. In time, as we served both male and female Soldiers, we'd explore a related theme: "Worth Knowing" with the guiding question of "What makes you worth knowing?"

In most instructional settings, it's helpful to know something of a person's background. I've been in many sessions when I knew basically nothing about the speaker and still only a little more than nothing when they were done. Some personal context helps. Too much can leave you wondering if the leader is going to get to the subject at hand. There is a tension there.

I tell the group something about where and how I grew up, marriage, children, interests, and challenges taken on in running, backpacking, parenting. It's kind of fun to ask a group what they would like to know.

"But you shouldn't listen to me because of any of that. You should listen to me because I've made more mistakes than you. And, I've tried to learn from those mistakes."

AT THIS POINT

Then the very first question of the very first instructional session often goes something like: I'd like you to think about a person from your past who influenced you to be the person you are today. This is someone you know personally. Not some famous actor or musician, or social media personality. Who is that person who influenced you to be the person you are today and did so in a significant way?

So who came to your mind?

Would you take a few moments to make some notes in the margin of this chapter?

Finally, if it aligns with your own faith tradition, would you think about the passage of Scripture below as you think about what most people value in this life?

> Therefore I tell you, do not worry about your life, what you will eat or drink; or about your body, what you will wear. Is not life more than food, and the body more than clothes? Look at the birds of the air; they do not sow or reap or store away in barns, and yet your heavenly Father feeds them. Are you not much more valuable than they? Can any one of you by worrying add a single hour to your life?
>
> And why do you worry about clothes? See how the flowers of the field grow. They do not labor or spin. Yet I tell you that not even Solomon in all his splendor was dressed like one of these. If that is how God clothes the grass of the field, which is here today and tomorrow is thrown into the fire, will he not much more clothe you—you of little

AT THIS POINT

faith? So do not worry, saying, 'What shall we eat?' or 'What shall we drink?' or 'What shall we wear?' For the pagans run after all these things, and your heavenly Father knows that you need them. But seek first his kingdom and his righteousness, and all these things will be given to you as well. – Matthew 6:25-33

AT THIS POINT

Chapter 4
Reflection: Where I've Been

Whatever failures I have known, whatever errors I have committed, whatever follies I have witnessed in private and public life, have been the consequences of action without thought. – Bernard Baruch, American financier[1]

Think about such things . . . (Philippians 4:8)

    That influential person leaves a mark; physical, mental, emotional, social, spiritual or vocational. Maybe more than one.
    I still remember a Fort Bragg Soldier who, at that time, was assigned to U.S. Army John F. Kennedy Special Warfare Center and School. The group, totaling sixteen with their Chaplain, gathered on a large camp deck in western North Carolina. As we discussed those who influenced us to be the people we are today, he plainly proclaimed for the entire retreat group, "My dad is a son of a bitch. I know how to live my life because I don't do anything he did."
    For some, the person who most influenced them is not an admirable example to follow.

AT THIS POINT

"Where I am" is completely influenced by where I've been. Where you are is completely influenced by where you've been.

There are layers to where I have been and how it affects where I am. If things are a bit off "where I am," there may be a fairly simple solution. I may need food, water, sleep, or benefit from intimacy with my wife. Have you heard of being hangry? Snickers® has sold a lot of bars capitalizing on the idea.

Speaking of a lack of food and sleep, I've heard stories about the United States Army Ranger School, considered the Army's premier training in small units tactics and leadership. Even with the rigorous Ranger Physical Assessment, which requires students to "complete 49 push-ups, 59 sit-ups, a 5-mile run in 40 minutes, and 6 chin-ups," to get into school, graduation rates are somewhere between 42-50 percent.[2]

In an April 2020 Outside magazine article by Will Bardenwerper, "Army Ranger School Is a Laboratory of Human Endurance," Ranger Class 05-19 began late February with 363 Soldiers. 61 days later, the 195 graduates gathered at Fort Benning's Victory Pond, only 69 of whom went through without recycling one of the three phases. Their Ranger tab is then pinned on their uniform.[2,3]

I hear that Ranger students often fall into two categories — sleepy Ranger or hungry Ranger. From my outsider's viewpoint, sleepy Rangers long for sleep but it evades them. It captivates their thinking and becomes one of the most challenging aspects of the school. Mind you, Ranger candidates are pushed to exhaustion and beyond.

Hungry Rangers are entranced by the desire to eat and the lack of it. Food consumes their thinking. "Ranger students conduct about 20 hours of training per day, while consuming two or fewer

AT THIS POINT

meals daily totaling about 2,200 calories (9,200 kJ), with an average of 3.5 hours of sleep a day."[4] For the amount of work they're doing, it's just enough food. The hungry Ranger is hungry all the time.

Just a little more food or just a little more sleep may solve their longing. The demand of their training is to learn to function as well as they can under this deprivation. Ranger candidates are learning to do more than they thought they could with less than they thought.

Food and sleep are important. Both. Not getting enough sleep or enough food can have adverse effects on our health over time. Too much food or too much sleep are also not good life strategies.

In the wisdom literature of the Bible, Proverbs 6:9 prods, "How long will you lie there, you sluggard? When will you get up from your sleep?" A sluggard is a habitually lazy person, not someone who needs more sleep.

Young parents can learn to care for their newborn child with less sleep. Medical residents are pushed to get their minds in gear on little sleep, in order to make an accurate diagnosis. We can do with less sleep. It's evident that many could do with less food. It's also statistically accurate that far too many do not have enough food on a daily basis.

There is a tension between "too much" and "not enough."

We, too, can learn to do without one or both, for a season, and become a stronger person as a result.

It's healthy to consider what appetites master us. Giving careful thought to those influences will help us better understand where we are.

AT THIS POINT

Influential Person

Think about that person again who influenced you to be the person you are today. What was it or is it about this person who influenced you? What did they say? What did they do? What was their most prominent character trait?

Hopefully, there is more than one person who came to your mind who influenced you well. For the purposes of this exercise, get one person clearly in your mind. Now, focus on these three questions: Who are they? How did they influence you? What was their occupation?

I've led sessions with male Soldiers who could not name a single man who influenced them well as they grew up. Not one. It's heartbreaking. I am so thankful for the women in those young men's lives who influenced them well: mother, grandmother, aunt, teacher, coach, and others.

Remember, I reflect on the past to see where I came from and how I got here, the present. The people who influenced me affect my present.

My choices also influence my present.

I recently read a story about a college football quarterback who was sitting with a group around a large table as a part of the TV show Below Deck. The racy photo shows a partially unclothed model with carefully placed leaves to make the story titillating. According to his own Twitter post, December 7, 2020, "It was not my idea nor any of my friends' ideas to eat sushi off of a model. I should have exercised better judgment and declined the idea immediately when it was brought up by the producers. This is not

AT THIS POINT

a reflection of my character or the way I was raised nor a reflection of the culture of UNLV Football."[5]

Pretty good apology. I'm trying to take him at his word. I think I am also hearing him try to say, "This is not who I am."

The truth is, that is exactly who he was, at that moment. At the time, he thought it was a good enough idea.

Before you think I am throwing him under the bus, please consider this. Have you ever gotten caught up in the moment which led into something you normally wouldn't do? I have. Have I done things that I hope never come to light? Yes. Would I like to deflect and say, "That's not who I am?" Yes.

The truth is, that is exactly who I was, at that moment. I may not want it to be so, but it is. If you have done something that you wish you had not done, it may not be who you want to be, but it is who you are at that moment. Look that in the eye. What is true?

Conclusion

Slowing down and looking at our past may be helpful. If it's settled and nothing is raising its head, then leave it alone. Don't look for something if nothing is there. But if there is something that recurs, it's time to face it.

The Bible encourages reflection but never uses the specific word. Synonyms like "consider," "think about," and "remember" pop up frequently instead.

When we practice honest reflection, it may take personal courage. Reflection can be hard. And if a person is unwilling and unable to look honestly at their past to see how it influences their present, that person is, if I may be so bold as to say, a coward.

AT THIS POINT

Often in an instructional session, participants are asked to shout out the occupation of the person who influenced them to be the person they are today. It's always a wonderful list. Here's the list from a February 2020 retreat: teacher, HVAC tech, salesman, engineer, waitress, food & beverage manager, politician, analyst, plumber, counselor, branch manager, unemployed, military leader, spouse, mechanic.

You see, it's not just the "influencers" who influence. People from all walks of vocational life significantly influence other people. And in case you haven't figured out that I am not Pollyanna[1], some influencers have influenced people in horrifically detrimental ways. We do not have to be adversely controlled by our past. It doesn't have to master your life.

To have been poorly influenced in the past does not have to leave you to the effects of that past. In order to be healthier, each of us can learn to reflect and "self-debrief" what has happened to us as well as the choices we make ourselves. I encourage you to look back at BENCHMARK's R3 6x6 self-assessment at the end of chapter three.

There is hope. Men who had poor male influence in the past can be men who influence others in profoundly impactful and significantly positive ways in the future. Women who had poor female influence from the past can be women who influence others in profoundly impactful and significantly positive ways in the future.

There are reasons why you are where you are. It may be simple or complex. Some actions and attitudes can be better controlled with some adequate food or sleep, until we better learn how to manage our actions with less. That's called maturity.

AT THIS POINT

Is there unresolved hurt? Or perhaps you have difficulty celebrating with joy the moments that really should be celebrated. Please, see what's going on in your past and learn from it.

In light of where you are and where you've been, determine where you want to go. You don't have to be the same person you have been.

What we choose to refocus on will set us off in a new direction.

Do you get adequate sleep?
Are you in a season of life when those limits are being stretched?
Do you eat well? Too much? Not enough?
Are your appetites your god?

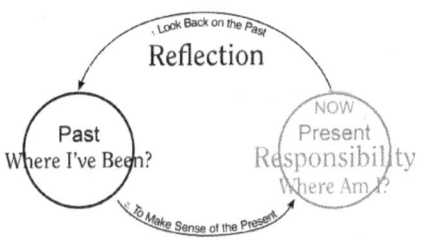

AT THIS POINT

Hit by a Truck

Before I began kindergarten, my family moved four and a half miles out of town to Route 2 Box 289 on two acres of land a mile and a half from the state highway. Jesup, Georgia, had a population of about 9,000, the county seat of Wayne County with a population of 20,000 at the time when I grew up there. When 911 became available, our road became Holmesville Road.

On Monday, January 21st, Mama and I rode bikes together on a three-quarter mile long, straight section of asphalt in front of our house. My bike was bright blue with a sparkly silver banana seat. It was a fun bike ride.

Tuesday after school, she let me ride by myself a quarter of a mile to my friend's house to play. January 22, 1974, became a day that changed my life.

I remember a car passing me. I remember moving to the left. I remember seeing the grill of a vehicle and that fast, blurry spinning just like you'd see in the movies.

Later I was told that while I was riding down the right side of the road, a car sped past me so closely it created enough of a vortex to pull me into the path of an oncoming pickup truck. Gene Rigdon, a neighbor who lived further down the road, did everything he could do to keep from hitting me. I was told he measured what was about to happen to me. He thought that if he went behind me to the right he would bat me down the road. He decided to go with me to the left, hoping he'd knock me off the road.

Laying on the side of the ditch, I could see Mr. Rigdon climbing out of his overturned truck which was now pointing the opposite

AT THIS POINT

way from its original direction. I was a bit bewildered by the whole thing, not understanding what had happened.

It's a weird thing to see a part of your body like you've never seen it before, seeing more of the inside of my leg than I ever wanted to. There wasn't much blood that I remember.

Mama heard a ruckus and came down the road where I was lying. She could only see a sheet covering all she could see of me. She thought I was dead. We were both in tears by the time she saw my face.

Mama and Daddy had stopped smoking sometime before, but Mama said that on that day, if she had a cigarette as long as her arm, she would have smoked it.

My hospital discharge summary reads, "This is an eleven-year-old white male who was doing well, prior to being run over by a truck on the night of admission."

Some people wonder what's wrong with me. Well, now you know. I was hit by a truck.

My first ambulance ride took me to the ER. All the damage was below my waist and predominantly to my right leg with multiple abrasions, and contusions. The right knee was the severest injury with all the skin peeled off my kneecap like someone had peeled an orange. I also had a partial tear of the patella ligament and broke my right ankle.

My first operation was an "extensive debridement of the right knee, including suture of the patella ligament & primary suture of the avulsed skin overlying the knee."

I woke with a full-length cast on my right leg and a window cut-out so the knee could be cared for.

Mr. Rigdon and I were both in our small-town hospital. I remember seeing him walk past my room one day, but he didn't

AT THIS POINT

come in. Though my family had no animosity toward him, I heard this accident affected him deeply.

So, there I was. Hanging out. A boy who rarely slowed down was slowed down.

My parents took turns most nights sleeping in my room. Friends of my parents, including adults from church, and school friends came to check on me, an advantage to being in a small town.

I was bored so my parents helped me to figure out what to do with the time. I made macramé flowerpot hangers with jute and colored wooden beads and sometimes empty plastic syringes as decoration. I created sand art, coloring salt with chalk and pouring it in glass jars to create beach and coastal bird designs. I think I even sold them.

Nurses would wake me up to ask me if I was sleeping well.

I have this distinct memory of a lab tech who somehow thought it was a good idea for him to sneak into my room to draw some blood while I was asleep. That didn't go well, for either of us. I don't think he ever tried again.

I learned about physical pain. As some of the reattached skin began to die, a doctor assisted by a nurse would pick away the dead and dying skin from around the knee until they reached pinkish skin. The knee was a mess. I'd hold onto a white rabbit pelt with one hand squeezing two of my daddy's fingers with the other while biting a blanket. They had to clear away whatever they thought would impede healing, but I wasn't happy about it.

There is a reason why the nonprofit ministry I founded is not called BENCHMARK Ministries. The benchmark symbol on a topographic map can have the subscript of BM beside it. However, the abbreviation BM reminds me of when I was that 11-year-old boy in the hospital. The nurses would come and ask if I

AT THIS POINT

had had a bowel movement. A "BM." Nope, BM wouldn't work for an abbreviation. Nor are we called BAM! because other nonprofits use that acronym and we're not a subsidiary of the Emeril Lagassé restaurant empire. We're BENCHMARK Adventure Ministries, aka BENCHMARK, not BM!

With an open wound over my knee and skin needing to cover it, my second surgery was a split thickness graft with skin from my left thigh used as cover on my right knee where the skin didn't survive.

I was in the hospital for 28 days.

There was no professional physical therapy in the piney woods of south Georgia. Mama was my physical therapist. I had to learn to put pressure on that knee again, with a casted ankle. She worked to get as much movement back into that knee as she could. It was unpleasant. I had to learn to walk again.

When I was up to it, a teacher came to our house with my school assignments. After being out of school for three months I returned to middle school a little ahead of where other students were with that cast still on my right ankle.

As an adult, I learned that my right leg is a little shorter than my left which has tilted my pelvis, exacerbating some periodic disc issues in my lower back.

I was a twelve-year-old who didn't sit still, but the skin on my knee was too thin for an active boy. I wore a Telfa pad often since I'd tear open the skin on my knee regularly.

Life resumed as normal as it could. I went to Boy Scout camp, church camp, hunted, fished, worked in our yard, and resumed baseball when my parents would let me. Coach Thornton was afraid I would reinjure myself so he didn't play me. I didn't have the same concern and was upset I didn't get to play more. In time

AT THIS POINT

I was behind the plate again as the catcher for the Tigers. Willie was the most impressive pitcher of any team in our town. I caught Willie. I think I was a pretty good catcher for our team, but my skills were outpaced by other boys by the time I got to high school.

In April of 1977 I did something to my fifth metatarsal in my left foot which required a cast. Nine days later they replaced the pedestal walking cast heel. Five days later it was replaced again. A week after that the cast was removed. I simply wore the heels off.

The summer of 1977 would be full. It was my brother's high school graduation, but I didn't attend it, being allowed to take my first trip aboard a small oil tanker with my Uncle Ken Casson who was the chief engineer. My parents drove me to Tampa, Florida, to get on the ship to head to Texas. It was great fun. Everyone on the ship knew who I was but I worked on that ship. I ate in the officer's dining room only after asking permission to enter. I could go to the bridge anytime day or night when I wasn't working but had to asked permission to enter there, too. The whole thing was great fun.

I went back to Boy Scout camp, but I think I missed church camp. It was time to address the thin skin on my knee with another graph surgery, a pedicle flap. This procedure was done in Brunswick, a little bigger town that had better medical specialties about forty miles from Jesup.

The surgeon cut a flap of skin from my left calf, leaving it partially attached. Then, the flap from my left calf was stitched to cover my right knee. For a time, my calf and knee were both connected. The idea was to end up with live, fleshy skin on my knee. I hung out, literally, with my legs casted together for a week waiting to learn if the graph took.

AT THIS POINT

I had a number of professional medical visitors come by to view this not-often seen procedure. I made more macramé flowerpot hangers and more sand art.

After a week, and over the next two days, they would cut a third of the way through to test the skin's connection before taking me back to surgery to finalize it by stitching it all down.

When we went back to Brunswick for checkups, the treat was to go to an all you can eat Chinese buffet. Sometimes we'd visit some of my parents' friends, the Hendersons, who likely prayed for me and whose kids I went with to church camp.

Some months later, in the final consultation as the surgeon looked over his successful procedure, he counseled me that with the extent of damage to my knee I would likely develop arthritis.

I can still hear these words in my head as clearly today as I did all those years ago. I didn't say them out loud, but I thought, "Arthritis? It'll have to catch me."

That was my mindset. I was going to do what I could do as long as I could.

I played more baseball—somehow tore some cartilage in my chest when I tried out for basketball which I wasn't very good at—and earned the Eagle Scout through the Boy Scout troop. Frankly, I did whatever I could do.

Scars? I have a few. My right knee is still covered with skin from two other parts of my body. There are healed puncture wounds and road rash, large scars on the front and back of my left thigh and my left calf from where skin was surgically mined and put somewhere else on my body. My legs aren't pretty but they work pretty well.

Only by the kindness of God, good medical care, and a bit of hard-headedness, am I alive today and able to walk and run.

AT THIS POINT

I wasn't going to let getting hit by a truck keep me from doing what I was capable of. I still don't.

AT THIS POINT

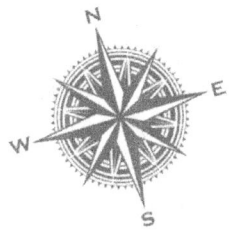

Chapter 5
Reflective Connections from My Faith Tradition

Everybody thinks of changing humanity and nobody thinks of changing himself. – Count Leo Tolstoy

If Christ comes to rule the hearts of men, it will be because we take him with us in the tractor, behind the desk, when we're making a sale to a customer, or when we're driving on the road. – Alexander Nunn

It ain't those parts of the Bible that I can't understand that bother me, it is the parts that I do understand. – Mark Twain

Grace is not opposed to effort; it is opposed to earning. Earning is an attitude. – Dallas Willard[1]

I pause every time I read or listen to Philippians 3:18-19:
"For, as I have often told you before and now tell you again even with tears, many live as enemies of the cross of Christ. Their destiny is destruction, their god is their

AT THIS POINT

stomach, and their glory is in their shame. Their mind is set on earthly things."

Can you hear the screech of the wheels when the mental brakes are slammed to the floor? "…their god is their stomach." Their appetites have become their god. Albert Barnes elaborates on this in his biblical commentary, defining Christ's enemies as those "who worship their own appetites; or who live not to adore and honor God, but for self-indulgence and sensual gratification"[2]

Paul, the writer to the church at Philippi, is telling a group of people in a church that their appetites had become their god. That's a sobering idea to consider. This passage gives me ample warning that I should contemplate what and who I am worshipping so that my appetites do not become my god. And I need to consider how they may be.

I also think of Peter, one of Jesus' closest followers while Jesus was on earth. Jesus predicted that Peter would throw Him under the bus. Peter was pretty sure it wasn't going to the case. He wasn't going to deny Him publicly. Mere hours later, it was true. Read this account in the Gospel of John 13:31-38, 18:15-27, 21:15-22.

Is this who Peter was at that moment?

Yes.

After Jesus' resurrection, He challenges Peter to realign himself to follow Him. The beauty of this is that Peter did not have to continue to be who he was. He could choose to change course and move in a better direction—forgiven.

And in one of my favorite/personally challenging interactions in all of Scripture, Peter is being Peter. John 21:21-22 gives us an account when Jesus tells Peter in clear terms the kind of death Peter would experience. He, again, not wanting to believe it will

AT THIS POINT

be true, chooses to deflect. He asks "Lord, what about him?" Peter does a little comparison and asks about someone else's future, to which Jesus clearly answers with a simple statement by the King of all Kings. "If I want him to remain alive until I return, what is that to you? You must follow me" (John 21:21-22).

I have stolen and lied and likely committed every other sin that falls under the categories of the lust of the flesh, the lust of the eyes, and the pride of life. Confession and repentance should look sin in the eye and say, "This is who I am. I am an imperfect, hardheaded follower of Jesus. This is what I did. I ask to be forgiven."

It's hard enough to learn from mistakes made in private even when I come to the realization that I was wrong. How much harder, in the day of "cancel culture," when the public mistake of a public figure is continuously talked over for a few news cycles for the purpose of increased ratings.

Grace

In my faith tradition, as a follower of Jesus Christ, when I repent by confessing my wrong and ask for forgiveness, I receive grace. Grace is beautiful.

I took a college level systematic theology course led by Mr. F. Leroy Forlines after I finished grad school. It's one I was able to avoid when I was actually in college. Some years later I wanted to hang out with college students while continuing to keep my mental and spiritual muscles moving. It was in that class that the biblical and theological foundations for BENCHMARK became clearer for me. I wonder if Mr. Forlines knew.

AT THIS POINT

His very simple, clear definition of people as thinking, feeling, and acting beings helps. We think with our minds, feel with our hearts, and act with our will. That set of three fits very nicely around the three sides of a triangular benchmark.

It's Forlines who defines grace as "God's love manifested toward the ill-deserved."[3]

With the small group that meets in our home, I'm in a study of the letter written by James to the scattered Jewish Christians outside of Israel. We're using James for You by Sam Allberry[4] as a guide. A couple of us are also reading Warren W. Wiersbe's classic, simple volume Be Mature, which defines grace as "God, in His grace, gives us what we do not deserve."[5]

Two points are key: one: It starts with God, His love for me, and two: I am not deserving.

This is not a question of my worth. I have been created in the image of God, completely loved and highly valued. But I do not deserve this grace. I am not entitled to it.

Because of the grace of God, my relationship with Him can be restored, made whole and connected.

Jesus told the story of a father and his two sons to help us to understand this idea of grace, and so much more. Parables give us the chance to see ourselves as a character in the story. You may be aware of the story of the younger son who asked his father for his inheritance. Often people call this the Prodigal Son. More specifically, it's in a set of three stories around the theme of "lost." This is the story of the lost son.

The younger son took his inheritance, left his father's house, and squandered his wealth in wild living. His lack of personal discipline and a famine in the whole country left him with nothing. This son no longer had his father's wealth to rely on. He found

AT THIS POINT

employment – in an embarrassing turn of events, this Jew was sent to feed pigs.

I particularly like the idea found in the words of Luke 15:17: "When he came to his senses." This young man had been doing reflection and based on his past choices and his current circumstances, he made a life changing decision. He decided to go back to his father's house with a willingness to be a hired servant.

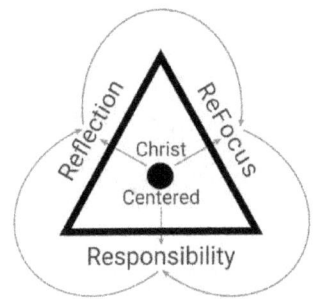

He looked his situation in the eye and didn't like what he saw. It took courage for this son to go back to his father's house, to face his older brother and his father's servants. That's coming to his senses.

And while I see myself most often as the older son in this story, it's vital to contemplate the father's response. "But while he was still a long way off, his father saw him and was filled with compassion for him; he ran to his son, threw his arms around him and kissed him." (Luke 15:20)

The father was watching for him; his love for his son compelled him to do so.

It was the son's need and just enough courage that put him close enough for the father to see him. The father was watching for him, His love for his son compelled him to do so. That's grace! The beauty of grace is that my past doesn't have to dictate my future.

AT THIS POINT

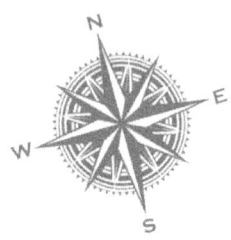

Chapter 6
Reflection toward Better Teams

Asking Questions to Build Better Teams

If you don't know where you are going, you'll probably end up somewhere else. – author unknown

MEETINGS: None of us is as dumb as all of us.
despair.com

A teacher who is attempting to teach without inspiring the pupil with a desire to learn is hammering on cold iron. – Horace Mann

Let he who would move the world, first move himself. – author unknown

Do or do not. There is no try. – Yoda, galactic philosopher

For many of BENCHMARK's years, we served groups of people who had some desire to be a team: people preparing for and then

AT THIS POINT

returning from a mission trip, middle school students, high school students, college students, volunteer staff, a few corporate groups, even leadership development of our own staff.

A particularly memorable training in 2018 allowed me the honor to travel on BENCHMARK's behalf to La Paz, Mexico, serving Rancho el Camino, an official ministry initiative of TEAM— The Evangelical Alliance Mission. The purpose given by Pete Johnson, Ranch co-director, was to help Mexican staff and American staff become Ranch Staff.

Rancho el Camino is twenty minutes outside the Baja California Sur's capital LaPaz, Mexico, and is a little over two hours north of Cabo San Lucas, three hours by shuttle van. This peninsula is a wonderful, extreme land of beauty, sand, clear water, wildlife, palm trees, critters, and cactus. Lots of cactus, 120 species of cactus. It's a remote location where medical care is not readily available.

The group of twelve people consisted of six Mexicans, six Americans; five females and seven males with a desire to build a relational community for God's glory and His honor.

I don't speak Spanish so Emily, the co-director, was given the unenviable task of translating my choppy, southern-dipped English.

After introductions we began the first day under an elegant palm frond thatched shelter. The group was briefed on the challenge and given some tarps to flip. Using what the ranch had available, the group started with a blue tarp and a smaller green one for just enough real estate. Without stepping off or touching the ground with any part of their body or clothing, the stakes increased. Now, turn it over. Over time and with success, the tarp size gets smaller. First the blue and then a pretty small green tarp.

AT THIS POINT

With experience and learning together, we can often take on more difficult challenges.

A simple rope to jump and a decreasing number of concrete blocks can be used to increase the demand for a group to foster cohesion.

Since Rancho el Camino is a working ranch, our sessions were interspersed within their regular responsibilities and even some restful recreation. Rest is as important as work.

Perhaps simple experiences with their thoughtful reflection helped Mexican staff and American staff become Ranch Staff.

For all of us, maturity and growth are a slow process. Perhaps the best we can hope for is short term improvement that may mature into longer term strategic team development.

Whether it's another country, across town, or somewhere in between, small group team building is oriented toward action/reflection. We do something and talk about it. We do something else and talk about it. Groups are led toward an appropriate tension to ready themselves to ask better questions. Some say that BENCHMARK has been "frustrating people since 1993." We even have a t-shirt that says so.

Small groups are given interactive, active, problem-solving tasks where it's helpful for them to define the problem, formulate solutions, and work together to accomplish them. It's most often helpful to think, communicate, listen, and act.

These initiative activities rely heavily on participant engagement. They are encouraged to "wade right in" to the experience, which will increase the likelihood for learning and personal growth.

AT THIS POINT

After giving some time to work on the challenge, I ask various versions of these two questions periodically throughout the training: What's working well? What's not working well?

The order doesn't matter as much as much getting at the ideas in both these questions. I want the questions to stick in their minds long after our time together has ended.

The underlying question, whether it is going well or not well, is: "Now, what are you going to do about it?"

If it's not working well, what are you going to do about it? If it is working well, what are you going to do about it?

Allow me to play with the ends of the spectrum.

If you are a person who is bent a particular way, you can most often see what you and others are doing very well. You're focused on the accomplishment, the completion, the success, the positive progress. You may be in a particularly good place for now. Celebrate it. Enjoy it. Repeat it, if at all possible.

That same person often has difficulty seeing the areas that need to be improved, corrected, or adjusted. They can be blind to their shortcomings or real difficulties. Have you heard of Pollyanna? The fictional character was an "excessively cheerful or optimistic person who just wants to pretend that all is sweetness and light."[1] To overwhelmingly live life with this bent, this tendency, and an inability to see what's not working well, will lead you to arrogance and delusion.

But if you are a person who is bent a different way, you readily see what you and others are not doing very well, what needs work: the "negative." You can clearly see what's wrong or at least what's not right. Perhaps you dwell on it too much. Some "team" dynamics are so out of whack that they should be pointed out, acknowledged, terminated, and then . . . mourned.

AT THIS POINT

That same person may find it difficult to celebrate progress, improvement, and growth. They are wading through the muck of it, and it's taking them down. To overwhelmingly live life with this bent will lead you to depression and delusion.

If you or your group are not in a particularly good place for now, try to see it as realistically as you can, with less drama and without turning it into an Instagram post.

The real adventurous journey is to learn to do both of these well, on an ongoing basis; celebration and mourning, progression and regression, benefits and detriments. Seeing both of those perspectives as clearly as you are able can be very helpful if the purpose is improvement. It's holding the ends of the spectrum in appropriate tension. Doing both may straighten out our tendencies with a viewpoint we don't normally take. That moves us to maturity and growth!

Looking carefully at what is working well and what is not working well can help you to realize that known place. From that known place, you can refocus on the shorter-term future and, then potentially, longer-term. Now that's a journey of personal courage.

AT THIS POINT

Chapter 7
ReFocus: Foundation

Am I now trying to win the approval of human beings, or of God? Or am I trying to please people? If I were still trying to please people, I would not be a servant of Christ. (Galatians 1:10)

Since then, you have been raised with Christ, set your hearts on things above, where Christ is, seated at the right hand of God. (Colossians 3:1)

The only ideas that will work are those we put to work.
– unknown

If you have courageously taken responsibility for as much as you can of where you are now, and courageously looked back on as much as you can of your past to better understand where you are now, then you are ready to courageously look to the future, as much as you can.

This third segment is a very important part of this ongoing cycle for life. Where I want to go is forward facing. It's the good 'F' word: Future. Remember that "re-" and the idea from the Aristotle praxis

AT THIS POINT

indicates repetition. In BENCHMARK's R3 toward Resilience framework, this is <u>Re</u>focus.

You're moving into the future every second. You might as well give some thought to where that's taking you.

I'm curious: If you stay on the path you're on, whatever that path is, will it take you where you want to go?

So, what path are you on? Would you set a timer on your phone and think about that for two minutes? Does your current path bring you joy, lasting joy? Do you keep repeating the same heartbreak with little hope for the future? What do you think? Will your current path take you where you want to go?

If I want to be a thoughtful person, I should consider how I want to live, to refocus not only on what I want to do but on who I want to be in the future.

This nonprofit ministry has a foundational Bible verse. It's even on our t-shirts. "Be very careful, then, how you live—not as unwise but as wise, making the most of every opportunity, because the days are evil." (Ephesians 5:15-16)

I've heard more than a few messages on Ephesians 5:15-16 and my interest is piqued when someone is presenting it. Most messages tend toward a micromanaging slant focusing on time, as if this passage is about time management in an overbearing way. I'm sure I've lived some of that out and pressured others to do the same.

But I've long thought that 15 and 16 are the pivotal verses of chapter 5. They have broad ramifications for all of life; a steady directive for me to be very careful how I live. Be wise. Live wise.

AT THIS POINT

Wisely make the most of every opportunity. Read through the Ephesians 5 and note the variety of topics that are addressed. While our use of time is a very important matter, wisdom for all of life is a greater one.

In early July 2016 I listened to a Your Move podcast by Andy Stanley entitled "Ask It." I highly anticipated his study of Ephesians 5 and was curious to learn how someone else understands these verses. I think he accurately gets at the heart of Ephesians 5 with his question, "In light of my past experience, my current circumstances and my future hopes and dreams, what's the wise thing for me to do?"[1]

Wisdom doesn't seem to be a high cultural value and there is not that much conversation about it. But it is a high biblical value. There is wisdom in the Holy Bible which can help me to take my next best step.

It's difficult to start at ReFocus without the background of Responsibility or Reflection. If you think you need to change or decide to stay the same, you've done reflection. If you are looking toward the future, you're doing reflection. When you do honest reflection, you have taken a step toward responsibility.

I've spent quite a bit of time in the woods doing navigation with a map and compass. The U.S. military calls it "land nav" for short. This valuable outdoor skill must be practiced in order to determine where you are by using a topographic map and a magnetic compass. In the twenty-first century, electronic GPS is extremely helpful. I use it regularly, but it doesn't always work in some of the places I find myself. And when I am in that kind of place, that's a good day for me.

Map and compass navigation is a critical element of the Ten Essentials developed in the 1930s by the Mountaineers who were

AT THIS POINT

early leaders in outdoor skills instruction. Those essentials are reiterated in the latest, ninth edition of Mountaineering: Freedom of the Hills.[2]

Daddy taught me my first practical land nav skills while deer and hog hunting in Fort Stewart in southeast Georgia. Back then civilians were allowed to hunt with a permit. He gave me a simple black plastic compass with a flip top cover to have with me anytime I was in the woods. It had a simple, twisted nylon string attached so I wouldn't lose it.

When in an unfamiliar area, we'd reference the map before we left the truck to see which direction the roads ran. Fort Stewart had all kinds of new roads, old roads, tank trails, fire breaks, and pig paths. My daddy was teaching me about orienteering "catching features" before I ever knew the term.

We climbed a lot of straight loblolly pine trees using the climbing tree seats Daddy had built. We'd get in our stand before daybreak and, after a midday break, again in the afternoon until it was so dark that I couldn't tell the difference between stumps and potential targets. If I got turned around (or maybe when) I needed to have the skill to get myself out of the woods and back to where someone could find me. I didn't have a cell phone. Bag phones weren't even a thing.

In Boy Scouts I practiced land nav by earning a skill award to loop onto my belt and the Orienteering merit badge. I was learning how to figure out where I was, what was around me, and how to get where I needed to be. Sound familiar?

In the summer of 1990, I was in the Wilderness Leadership Practicum training to become a wilderness instructor in the High Road program. At Honey Rock, the same Wheaton College camp I was doing a graduate school internship three years before in

AT THIS POINT

residential camp, I remember watching the High Road instructors come back from their land nav assessment. I wondered how I would do. Now, three years later, it was time to find out.

I had three hours to find seven points over a wide course. I was ready. I may have been overconfident.

It didn't go as well as I had hoped. Some I found quickly. A couple of others took over an hour each to find. The mental errors couldn't be overcome by my physical capabilities. I was 19 minutes over the cut off time.

I knew this skill. I had lost too much time. I was angry with myself.

I had another opportunity to make the cut, to improve. This was a critical skill I needed to know well.

It may have been the very next day when I had another chance to run the newly revised course. I started at 2:53pm, finding all seven points then running back to the finish to complete the course in fifty-seven minutes. I still remember the smile on my face.

I read the terrain better, picked up my pace, and crushed my previous time. Slowing down when I was uncertain, relying on my past experience, and moving quickly when confident made a difference too.

A small directional change can make a significant difference over time and distance. It helps to ReFocus on where I want to go.

What's the wise thing to do?

AT THIS POINT

AT THIS POINT

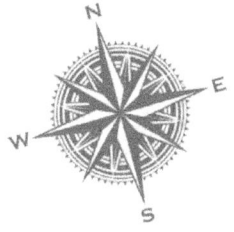

Chapter 8
ReFocus

Practice Leads to Change

People are so ready to think themselves changed when it is only their mood that is changed! – George MacDonald, *The Wise Woman*[1]

Character is not made in crisis—only exhibited.
– Robert Freeman

Doing right things is more important than doing things right. – author unknown

Some time ago, I was leading the ReFocus session with a group of elite aviators. I asked them, "How far off from where you want to be will you be if you are one degree off in 100 yards?"

"Sir, we don't use degrees." I was kindly corrected. "We use mils, and meters."

Mils are most often used in the U.S. military since it's a smaller increment and more accurate. None of our previous Chaplains Partnership Initiative military ministry event participants had

59

AT THIS POINT

corrected me. These men wanted me to be accurate, just like they have to be when they fly.

With a quick adjustment on my part, "How far from where you want to be will you be if you are one mil off in ten meters? One of the pilots paused for maybe a half a second and told me the exact distance between the two locations.

Surprised, and obviously under-skilled for this group, I asked, "Can you see where you want to be?"

"Probably."

"How far off would you be from when you want to be if you are one mil off in 100 meters?" Again, I was told the answer. "Can you see where you want to be?"

"Maybe; depends on the terrain." Heads were nodding up and down. The response was unanimous.

One thousand meters? Yes, they knew. Ten thousand meters? "Could you see where you should have been?"

"You're lost."

Trust me, in their world, "lost" would be a serious concern. There are grave consequences for other Soldiers when pilots are not where they are supposed to be.

The great news is that this can also work to our benefit. A small directional change can make a significant difference over time and distance. What if I adjust one degree today? What if I choose to make a healthier choice in any area of my life. Will anybody see the difference today? Doubtful.

What if I choose to be grateful a little more in the next week? Will anyone notice? Maybe.

What if you made the effort to reduce your "blame game?" You can decide today to take more and more responsibility for your own actions, attitudes . . . and emotions.

AT THIS POINT

What if you drastically reduced or ended an activity that is hampering your well-being and growth? What effect is your consumption of social media, daily news, alcohol, porn, TV, Netflix, food, sleep, selfishness, discontentment, blame, ingratitude, or self-medication of all kinds having on you? There also may be an enjoyable or beneficial activity that has too high of a priority in your life for this particular season of life.

My life is out of balance too. The idea of balance can make it sound like there is even the possibility of having the priorities of life in some weighted equality. All of the demands of life need to be held in appropriate tension.

Can you look carefully at the influences of your life and take a step to be the person you really want to be? What is out of appropriate tension, keeping you from being a healthier person relationally and personally? Which one sticks out to you?

Go to work on that one.

Will you be noticeably different in a month, three months, six months? Do you think anyone else will notice? Maybe.

Will you be becoming a different person? Definitely.

There is something more important than anyone actually noticing if you are a different person. It's that you will be in a much better place. You will be different. Your life will change.

"I need to remember..."

Have you been in an "instructional setting" of any kind and come upon an idea that you knew you needed to apply to your life?

When I was in school outside of Chicago in the late 1980s, I worshiped at Butterfield Community Church. We participated in a

AT THIS POINT

50 Day Spiritual Adventure produced by The Chapel of the Air. A critical part of the spiritual adventure was the End-of-the-Day Replay to daily ponder how I lived that day. Since it was connected to my faith tradition, I was to invite the Holy Spirit to walk with me through the events of the day to see it from that perspective. What interactions were joyful? Which ones did I need to re-address, ask forgiveness for, or improve?

Near the end of BENCHMARK's adventure retreats, participants are asked to think carefully about the events they have been involved in. The military does professional reflection regularly called an AAR: After Action Review.

It's not that I think that BENCHMARK is the most stellar adventure anyone has ever been on—but it is the most recent. It's a short period of time that a participant can wrap their mind and heart around the hours-long events or the day(s)-long events, long enough to think about but short enough to not overwhelm.

Based on the events and training, participants are asked to capture memories from the day through "I need to remember…" Yes, it's another opportunity for reflection. For all of us, it's a chance to consider what to repeat, celebrate; "what I should do again?" It's also a chance to contemplate what is to repent, criticize; "what I should not do again?" It's an idea that could make a lasting change to the course of our lives in the coming days if we take time to focus on it.

Here are some responses from 2020 Chaplains Partnership Initiative retreat participants. I need to remember…

"that achieving my goals is important, but my family is also important and keeping that bond is important."

"the truth hurts but it's the truth. Own up to it."

AT THIS POINT

"come back to this because this trip brought me back to God. Also strengthen bonds between my battle buddies."

Today you can decide who you want to become. Your past actions and attitude do not have to dictate how you will step into the future. Your past actions and attitude may influence where you are, but they do not have to dictate who you will be. You get to choose, today. Today, you can start being the person that you want to be.

What about your next best step?

I have looked carefully at what I have done, again. I have considered who I am, again. I have jotted down some ideas that I need to remember. I am ready to determine my next best step. What am I going to do now? The next best step is personal, hopeful, and loving.

What one thing will you focus on in the next few days, then weeks, that will make a significant life change for you?

Choose something to do that is in one of the wellness dimensions; physical, mental, emotional, social, spiritual or vocational. What specifically will you do?

In Refocus, I personally have taken steps to improve my journaling (mental, spiritual), flexibility (physical, emotional), listening to the Bible in a year (spiritual, mental), leading a small group (social, spiritual).

So...what will be your next best step?

AT THIS POINT

AT THIS POINT

Reject the worldly lie that says, That life lies always up ahead. – Michael Card[1]

Because of the LORD's great love we are not consumed, for his compassions never fail. They are new every morning; great is your faithfulness. (Lamentations 3:22-23)

Mama and Daddy

Our parents just are. Even if we know some things about where they grew up and their time together before we came along, it's as though they always were.

My mama grew up in Hinesville, Georgia. Her parents, Fannie Lou Edenfield and Lonnie Dunn, divorced before it was fashionable. Edna DeWees Dunn was the middle child with an older sister, Georgia Naomi, and one younger brother, James Lonnie. All three graduated from Bradwell Institute. As long as I knew, my grandmother, aka Bum Bum, worked in the office of the Liberty County Commissioner and lived with her sister and brother-in-law on the coast overlooking five miles of Georgia salt marsh.

Mama attended her fiftieth high school reunion and kept up with high school friends as long as she could.

Daddy was the son of a sharecropper from Statesboro, Georgia, with family roots all the way back to Wales. His mother, Lillie Mae, was one of the sweetest people I ever knew, a quiet woman with beautiful white hair and a pleasant smile. She made the best fried apple tarts.

AT THIS POINT

His dad, John Varnadoe, was quieter still, a craftsman, former finish carpenter back before there were many power tools. He knew more than a little bit about gardening. They could see the chickens under their house through the cracks in the floors.

My brother told me that because of a dispute with the landowner, Granddaddy went to Savannah to find work. My daddy and his brother Harold loaded their guns in case the property owner came by to give them a hard time. Granddaddy got work in the Savannah shipyard, and they moved there. Working there, Granddaddy got hurt pretty badly and that is why he limped. Grannie and Granddaddy both had challenging lives. She followed Jesus and went to church with us. He did not.

In Savannah, Daddy ran with boys around Forsyth Park and did odd jobs in the neighborhood. He told my brother that they cleaned windows for a lady who didn't pay them. They decided to go back with their slingshots and shoot some of her windows out.

Daddy told me about an altercation with a group of boys from a nearby neighborhood where he ended up on the short end of that event. He went home, got his slingshot, gathered some friends and rocks, then went and settled the matter. After that, they didn't have any trouble from the other group of boys.

I remember, too, that Daddy and Uncle Harold would take their guns on the city bus to go out somewhere to hunt birds to bring home for food.

A handsome man, Daddy left for the Navy when he was eighteen. One of his jobs was the machine gunner on a landing craft. Based on a coin toss between him and another guy, he didn't have to go though he was on a boat heading to Korea when that "conflict" ended. Honorably discharged as a Storekeeper Third

AT THIS POINT

Class after serving almost five years, he didn't tell many stories of his time in the Navy.

My parents married on September 2, 1955.

I understand they were kind of rough. My mama told my daddy, "If you ever lay a hand on me, don't lay down where I can find you." Did you catch that? She told my daddy that if he ever put his hands on her in anger, there would be consequences. That very clear declaration of boundaries still makes me smile. I'm pretty sure she could wield a cast iron frying pan. She never needed to.

Daddy worked at Western Auto in Savannah. Later they moved to northeast Atlanta where he earned his college degree from Southern Technical Institute while working full-time at Hastings Garden Center. They lived in a garage apartment on Lindbergh Road in Atlanta. His routine between work and school was such that he ordered the same thing from the same restaurant every day. Eventually they had his order waiting on him when he arrived.

He became an engineer doing bridge work for the Georgia Highway Department. When I was younger, there was a bridge we'd cross from time to time on Highway 17 near Richmond Hill, Georgia. He had worked on it early in his career. He was proud that for twenty plus years that bridge was still smooth all the way across. He became an engineering auditor with the Georgia Department of Transportation who could add a whole bunch of numbers in his head, finding the anomalies, something he could still do within days of his passing.

They found their way to Jesup, Georgia. So did a Free Will Baptist preacher who came to start a church in that small south Georgia town. J.E. Blanton sold insurance to help provide for his family and as a way to get to know people in the community. His wife Jean was a nurse.

AT THIS POINT

The preacher periodically knocked on my parents' front door. When my mama went to the front door to answer it, my daddy went out the back door. He wasn't going to have anything to do with it. But in time, my daddy did commit his life to Christ. My mama too. My life is different because of that decision, that commitment.

My brother and I were both born in Savannah, Georgia, which apparently meant a sixty-five-mile drive to the hospital. Daddy said to me, "If you had been the first, there wouldn't have been a second." Seems I was a handful even when I was young.

Mama called me "Tink." I answered to it because my mama was calling me, but I didn't understand it for a long time. Seems it's short for the fictional character Tinkerbell from Peter Pan who flitted around here and there.

Mama was a stay-at-home mom until I was older, then she worked in the public school so she could be home when my brother and I got home. Later she worked in an insurance office and spent fifteen years as an ombudsman, a liaison for the state of Georgia settling complaints between residents of nursing and personal care homes, and the facility management. If something wasn't right in one of those facilities, my mama was going to work to make it right for the resident.

She had seen too many of them to ever want to end up in one.

Mama traveled thirteen counties in southeast Georgia, sometimes into the evenings. She came home one evening still a bit jittery. While driving home on the country roads, a pickup truck had come right up behind her with headlights glaring into the car. For her, the truck was too close. She sped up a bit. So did the truck. She slowed down. So did the truck. In time, she reached under the center console, pulled out a 9mm Glock 26 holding the

AT THIS POINT

gun up toward the roof in clear view of the driver. Apparently, the pickup truck driver decided he could give my mama a little more room.

Mama would say, "Don't ask me my opinion and then argue with me about it." She wasn't opposed to people having a conversation after they had asked her opinion. She didn't like the "Tell me what you think" which was followed by "Now DeWees, you know…" or "Are you sure you…"

Daddy enjoyed hunting and fishing. Every Saturday between October 15 and the first weekend of January, my daddy was going to be in the woods hunting deer and hogs. There were other Saturdays spent hunting turkey, quail, and dove. When my brother and I were old enough, he taught us to hunt, to respect other people's land, not to waste what we harvested, and to follow the law.

They both served in the local church because of their commitment to Jesus Christ. Mama served in the nursery, was the Sunday school secretary for a time, and stayed involved in the women's auxiliary. I remember Daddy leading the youth program on Wednesday nights; he taught Sunday School and became a part of the church leadership as a deacon.

They were nominated to become members of the Gideons International, which is most widely known for distributing free Bibles in lodging rooms but also offered to military personnel, hospitals, nursing homes, prisons, and students. They grew in their commitment of faith through serving with people from other evangelical churches. They considered it a high honor to be a Gideon.

AT THIS POINT

 Daddy, with Mama, made decisions based on the convictions of their faith, choosing not to hobnob after work. This decision likely affected his job promotions.
 Daddy's idea of "fun" was an acre garden. Each row was 100 feet long. Daddy made a plan and wrote it down, adjusting it annually. He was an early adopter of organic gardening and practiced crop rotation. The garden was divided into sevenths so that each year a one-seventh of the plot was allowed to rest. It was biblical.[2]
 If I could find his list it would be more accurate than my memory. It was something like six rows of string beans, eight rows of corn, six rows of tomatoes, six rows of Irish potatoes, plus mustard and turnips, bell peppers, jalapeños peppers, yellow squash, onions, Seminole peas, butter beans, eggplant, cabbage, okra, carrots, sweet potatoes. Then, it seemed like the list started over, repeating everything that was already planted.
 That garden was where I first started taking steps toward taking responsibility, doing what I was told (most of the time) even when I really didn't want to do it. South Georgia summers are hot. My daddy's parents worked the garden too. It wasn't just "fun," it's how we ate.
 My brother and I were both in Boy Scouts and Little League baseball; we cleaned the church for money.
 Mama and Daddy took care of relatives as they aged and passed, never asking for a thing in return. It's just what family does.
 Soon after my parent's fiftieth anniversary, my mama began to be affected by dementia, that slow slipping away of the person she was toward a person who didn't remember who she was.
 In time, my daddy took my mama's drivers' license away and her keys. He decided to revoke her Second Amendment rights

AT THIS POINT

too. He bought a bigger TV because he was going to be watching more of it since he didn't want to leave her and, at other times, couldn't leave her alone for long.

Daddy's periodic anger was seen when we'd visit. His wife of fifty-plus years was slipping away and the inability to reason with his once capable wife was difficult to bear.

In my mama's decline, my daddy still talked to J.E. Blanton periodically. Brother J.E. spoke at my daddy's funeral. My family benefited from a pastor who took time to pastor those in his congregation.

My brother and I, among others, offered to help, but he wouldn't accept much help. He didn't want to "inconvenience" his family. He shouldered the load, much more than he should, but wouldn't have it any other way.

He made a commitment to my mama and was going to see it through.

During my daddy's third bout with melanoma, the most serious type of skin cancer, a dear friend and neighbor alerted my brother and me that our parents needed support. My brother went first. Daddy finally allowed us to make arrangements for Mama to be cared for in a memory care center, for a short period of time, so he could focus on taking care of himself. For Mama, memory care was a misnomer. I then stayed with my parents, as my brother worked on the paperwork for the facility that he and Daddy had visited before.

The last night they were together, we sat in their living room. My mama sat on the couch with me, Daddy in his chair. She asked the same three questions for what seemed to be hours.

"Where's John?"

AT THIS POINT

He was right in his chair, feet away from her, yet she didn't know who he was. Of course she didn't know who I was either.

"When can I go home?"

She was sitting in the living room of the home she and Daddy built on the Georgia coast ten years before.

"When are we going to eat?"

We've already eaten. Would you like something else to eat?

That was Wednesday night. My brother came down on Thursday morning to take our mama to the memory care center so that Daddy could focus on his own care and cancer treatment.

As my daddy lay in bed to rest, I sat in their bedroom as we cried and laughed.

Thirteen days later, my daddy passed from this life to the next. They were married sixty years and a month.

Mama continued to slowly decline over the next few years. My brother and I had our feet under whatever table our mama had her feet under for Thanksgiving from the time we were born till she died.

In 2019 the facility needed to move the residents inland because of a threatening hurricane. She didn't make that move well. I went to south Georgia on Wednesday. After moving her back to the facility on Thursday, the hospice nurse's assessment was that she would likely pass within 24-72 hours.

I sat playing hymns from YouTube for Mama to hear. I was content that she would soon be with Daddy, her husband of sixty years, and that she had a relationship with Jesus Christ that would make that possible. That relationship changed her life…and mine.

We prayed her passing would be peaceful and that we would joyfully accept God's timing into the hands of the God she loved and served since before I was born.

AT THIS POINT

Then, with my brother and me near, she breathed her last.

Their cemetery slabs read:

> Mama, Edna DeWees Dunn, born Wednesday July 19, 1935, died Sunday September 8, 2019. Homemaker, Artisan, Steadfast Elder Advocate, Faithful Wife, Mother, and Grandmother. Well Done, Good and Faithful Servant.

She was 84 years old.

> Daddy, John Bridger Evans, born Wednesday September 25, 1929, died Wednesday October 7, 2015. Farmer, Sailor, Engineer, Devoted Husband, Father, Grandfather. A Gideon, and Christian Man of Stubborn Integrity.

He was 86 years old.

Many tombstones simply note the breadth of life that was with a hyphen, a dash; year of birth, dash, year of death. Just a small mark, the dash on a slab of stone captures an entire human life. Others have written about the significance of how we choose to fill the dash.

What I saw over time was two people whose commitment to each other and to the God they served deepened over time. I watched two people doing what was right and honorable, living out their values and trying to teach their sons to do the same. They cared about other people, shouldered the difficulties of other

AT THIS POINT

relatives, up to a point, and made a difference in the lives of those people, especially their immediate family.

I see a story of great beauty. I see an admirable legacy. I see their personal growth over time. I see family commitment and love for others that increased over time. I see people who stepped toward difficult circumstances, together.

I watched my daddy fulfill the vows he made to my mama years before. He honored that commitment to her till he could no longer.

It is that example that guides who I am and who I want to be when I grow up.

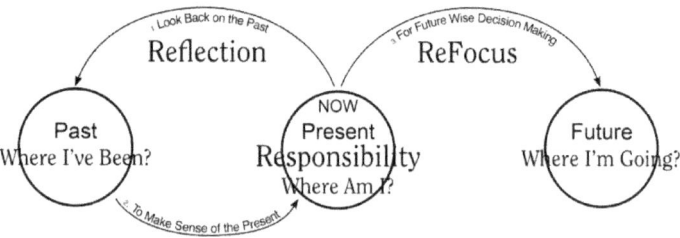

AT THIS POINT

Reflection Toward a Resilient Life
Part 2

A gathering of blogs, articles, workshop presentations and reflections over time, at a particular point in time, developed from the very integrative process that our participants are led to engage. This is my thinking at this point, presented chronologically. Perhaps what I've wrestled with will benefit you as you wrestle with your circumstances.

AT THIS POINT

 1989
I Still Remember

Vicky asks me to visit him with her. "He's a coworker's son," is all she says.

The day arrives to visit. We drive past trashy yards. The neighborhood's rough. All the houses are just alike, past the houses to where he lives in a high-rise owned by the city.

We are introduced. His name is Derrick.

The elevator takes us up. The view vast, his apartment small. Only four rooms, scantily furnished. The kitchen's akin to a closet.

Vicky and Derrick talk for an hour. I add to the conversation occasionally, feeling out of place, not really knowing my reason for visiting. I note his speech, who he talks about, and how he reacts to particular names. What we talk about always gives insight into who we are. He seems a bit uneasy. Me too.

As we leave, Derrick invites me to visit again. I tell him I will try. Days later Vicky tells me how much the visit meant to him...and his mom.

I phone irregularly, but see him less. Not many people call. Derrick's lonely, and he's thrilled to hear my voice. Slowly he is being cut off from all his friends.

During a visit he asks, "Do you know that I'm gay?"

"Yes, I do."

"How do you know? Did Vicky tell you?"

"No, I just figured it out."

In his living room he quizzes me about why his friends were slowly dying one by one. It doesn't make sense to him that a loving God would allow such horrible things to happen. I probe

AT THIS POINT

his relationship to God as he questions God's goodness. But, in my mind it is a fierce battle.

Uncompromising sermons scream. "They got what they deserved." Maybe. "Homosexuals go to hell." Yes, they do, but so do liars and gluttons. But how do I communicate God's holiness to Derrick in a way fitting that same loving God?

I got to know Derrick for about a year and a half, never being quite sure if my witness was appropriate. Once we feasted at McDonald's. He loves McDonald's, though he rarely eats there. His health is failing.

The last time I visited Derrick was at Vanderbilt Medical Center. Lights, tubes, and smells. We discussed his weakening and chatted about music. He never told me he had AIDS. We listen together to the Wayne Watson, Sandi Patty duet "Another Time, Another Place." He mouthed the words as his confession:

> And though I've put my trust in him
> And felt his spirit move in my life
> I know it's truly just a taste
> Of his glory in another place
>
> (Chorus)
> So I'm waiting for another time and another place
> Where all my hopes and dreams will be captured
> With one look at Jesus face
> Oh, my hearts been burnin'
> My soul keeps yearnin'
> Sometimes I can't hardly wait
> For that sweet sweet someday
> When I'll be swept away

AT THIS POINT

To another time and another place[1]

A few days later, I drove to the funeral home to pay my respects. Arriving uncomfortably, I find a seat quickly just inside the door. As I wait for his send off to begin a lady walks right up to me from across the room.

"Are you James?"

Shocked, I stammered, "Yes, I am."

"Your visits meant so much to Derrick. He enjoyed your talks."

Ashamed I sat, as tears moistened my eyes, for I knew how often I had visited. Even in my reluctance, God had used me to reach out to Derrick. My friendship was meaningful. My witness was useful in the hands of the Master.

The minister spoke of Derrick's recommitment and increasing faith in God. It's plain to me now, to this day, when I hear "Another Time, Another Place," I think of Derrick.

I still remember.

AT THIS POINT

⚠ **April 10, 2009**
What Soup Do You Swim In?: A Taste of Today's Culture

Recently I was a part of an outreach to backpackers on the Appalachian Trail. This 2175-mile National Scenic Trail begins in Georgia and extends all the way to Maine. During the spring, about thirty-five people a day start this epic journey. Within the first thirty miles, about fifteen percent of those who start decide to quit.

I arrived in the area on Wednesday evening and my first miles were in the rain. I was pretty wet. But that wasn't the end of it. Thursday it rained. Friday it rained. Saturday it stormed. Sunday it rained only a little bit. Since I had dealt with wet feet for twice that long on a wilderness trip, these five days were a challenge but not a new level of difficulty.

Tasting the Soup

When things get difficult and uncomfortable, we are able to get accustomed to them and work our way through them. Because we are created in the image of God, we have been given the capacity to adapt to things that were at one time uncomfortable for us. It's called maturity. Not only does this idea of becoming accustomed to something hold true for difficult things, but it also holds true for things we shouldn't get used to. Culture is often one of those things.

Culture is like a soup; it has many ingredients. While some of those ingredients can be beneficial, perhaps there are parts of our

AT THIS POINT

culture, this soup we swim in, to which we should never grow accustomed.

Leaving a Bad Taste in Your Mouth

When I was a kid, I had white friends and black friends. That's how I thought about my friends. Now, my kids just have friends. The color of their friends' skin isn't an issue. That's a good shift in American culture. It's a good part of the soup.

But culture is also moving us in unhealthy directions. Culture often tries to "mature" you. Some parts of culture try to help you grow up by showing you images and sharing ideas that you have not yet developed the emotional and social capacity to comprehend, let alone the spiritual maturity. The tendency of culture often steers away from purity, holiness, and things that are God-honoring.

As we get older, it's very normal to push the limits, question the rules, and seek to make our own choices. While growing up and becoming your own person is good, sometimes those choices can leave us with horrible memories and realities that are difficult—if not almost impossible—to shake.

For instance, look at Britney Spears. She is a cultural icon. Even with her troubles and decline over the past few years she remains a top Yahoo! search. With the release of Circus last fall, she proved she has what it takes to remain a major cultural force, and she continues to push the limits. Current icons such as Spears and Flo Rida have released songs whose hidden messages tend to slide right past most of us, but at their core, the songs devalue and dishonor God's plan for sexuality.

AT THIS POINT

I expect the intended audience for artists such as these do hear the messages loud and clear, but even if they don't, these songs and those similar to them are leading us in a direction to which we should not become accustomed. We are being trained. God created sexual expression with boundaries, but our current cultural evolution encourages a what-I-want, when-I want-it, and with-whomever-I-want-it attitude. This is not a good part of the soup.

If pop or hip-hop is not your style of music, pay close attention to how rock, metal, R&B and even country communicate a similar message. If we have to hear and understand these sexual messages before we can conclude the songs are not in line with God's character, perhaps we already have become accustomed to things we should not.

Failing to Recognize the Flavors

The bad parts of culture soup extend much further than current, popular music. The level of familiarity with pornography in our culture is astounding. Jay Leno's monologue often has references to pornography. Give some thought to the humor themes of Saturday Night Live, Scrubs, or dozens of other shows. While we may agree this influence is less than God-honoring, we may hear it so much that we become less bothered by it, or perhaps even immune, and yet another harmful ingredient is slipped unknowingly into the cultural soup.

There's no need to run and hide. We are in this world. This is the life we are to live. There are so many wonderful and enjoyable ingredients in our cultural soup, but there are also ingredients of this soup that hamper and hurt. The trick is not allowing these influences to overcome us.

AT THIS POINT

If you haven't noticed, homosexuality is mainstream. It has risen to be cool and classy, hip and happening. In addition, bi-sexuality is much more "normal" than in years past. Neither is new. These sinful tendencies have been a part of human life for a long time. It's part of pushing the limits and questioning the rules given by the One who is greater than humans. These choices are not a part of a God-honoring life. This is not a good part of the soup.

A fairly new addition to the soup is sexting. This new mode of "fun" is bursting on the electronic and social networking scene with damaging consequences. In just a moment, a single image can be seen worldwide. Those images may never go away, even if you want them to. The consequences are devastating.

While I am concerned about those influences that lead us away from God, I am also concerned about those who simply write Him out. Look around to see how much God is ignored in our culture. Many forms of entertainment (movies, songs, viral videos, TV programs, etc.) write God out of the script. He simply isn't an influence. Our culture makes an effort not to talk about Him because it might be offensive to someone who doesn't agree with those beliefs. This is not a good part of the soup.

We certainly are at liberty to enjoy things that don't necessarily use God's name. But let's not be so simplistic that we fail to acknowledge the fact that just because God is called by name doesn't mean He is honored.

Another cultural tendency is to overvalue fame. In fact, many people are willing to do most anything to gain it. In our culture, reality shows abound. The desire of teenagers and adults to be famous appears to short-circuit all rational thought and, for some, any connection with right and wrong. The funny thing is, these

AT THIS POINT

people, who don't even deserve our attention, are the ones our culture and media tend to follow most closely.

While being famous is not wrong, making fame the purpose of your life is. Even in the church's subculture, the desire to be famous pervades. Some of us do not live for God's name and His renown; we live for our own. What is your motivation behind updating Facebook or Twitter? Is it to develop healthy, honorable relationships with others, or is it because you want the focus to be on you? This desire to be famous, to be known, leads us in directions we shouldn't become accustomed to. It's not a good part of the soup.

A Bitter Taste Test

Some parts of our media and entertainment portray followers of Christ, or "church people," as stupid, weak, unloving and judgmental. While some Christians have provided good evidence that this is the case, a steady diet of those ideas will lead us away from God and His best for us.

All those things—being stupid, weak, unloving, and judgmental—may be true at one time or another in my life and perhaps yours, but society tends to elevate those traits and write off any valuable contributions followers of Christ make to culture. Those who seek His name and renown, those who lead people to a life of freedom in Christ, those who care for the poor and widows, and those who seek justice, love, and mercy are ignored or forgotten. We do well when we recognize that the One we are to honor with all of our life is being left out of the conversation of life.

AT THIS POINT

What Are You Swimming In?

So this is a bit of the soup we swim in. What's a person to do? We need to have the content filters of our lives fully engaged. All the time. We need to consider all of life in light of the character of God. He is holy. Is our music? He is loving. Does the TV we watch help us to be more or less loving? He is right and hates evil. Is evil our entertainment? God is great, grand, and forgiving. Does our media make us small, whiney, and selfish? He is creative. Do the movies we watch move us to be more or less creative?

Each of us needs to become more thoughtfully aware of the cultural influences that affect us. If your desire is to please Christ and to walk with Him, your guidance should be firmly based in God's Word. All of life, including our entertainment, relationships, and pastimes, should be viewed in light of the character of God in order to test its worthiness. Some of this soup can lead us to follow Christ and God's character with increased maturity. Some of this can lead us into a life of bondage and continued self-focus.

What are you swimming in? Is it good soup…or sewage?[1]

AT THIS POINT

 August 29, 2009 6:00am
Before I ~~Loose~~ Lose My Mind

    A new journey has begun. I think, I think it has begun. Perhaps it's just fear. But perhaps it's the truth.
    After a challenging run yesterday afternoon on the roads and trails of Edwin Warner Park, I am awake entirely too early. Ideas spinning in my head. It's the lack of clarity of thought late yesterday. The "I can't remember" and knowing that it's true.
    It's also the recollection that very often God had led my thoughts to clarity by helping to put this or that idea, and this or that life experience together in some coherent flow.
    Or this may just be fear. It may just be doubt snuck into my life by the adversary whose desire it is to rob and to destroy.
    The note my mama wrote in her seventies comes to mind. She stuck it on their refrigerator.

> "Dear God, in the name
> of Christ Jesus Would
> you please replace
> my memory that the
> Locus(t) have eaten and
> I thank you Dear Jesus
> in your name I pray
> Amen"

    I'm entirely too much like my mama. The family legacy of her mom. It may well be a long goodbye.
    I picked up Hannah from Hazel's birthday party. Some names, got them. Others, not so much. But I had remembered Allison's

AT THIS POINT

name earlier. Remembered Joe's and Cynthia's and Winston's. Weary mind or something else?

Barbara, my wife, hates it when I say it, but for a few years I've been saying "Ten good years." Or "Eight good years." Or less? It will be what it will be. I'll approach this journey much like I have the other forty-plus years of my life.

With tenacity. With fight. With resistance to go in a direction that I don't really want to go. Perhaps with anger. Maybe resentment. All those emotions I have lived out full bore, and sometimes hanging onto them for too many . . . months . . . years. But perhaps, too, there will be an abiding peace. With most years, certainly not all of my life, there has been an underlying trust, commitment, and desire to please only the One who gave me life.

So why am I writing? I want to leave my children and my wife a gift. I want to share with them this journey, though they will not hear all of it while I can still contain my thoughts. I want them to see their imperfect husband and dad . . . struggling. To let them know that I didn't go easily. That I didn't go without a fight. That their lives matter to me and that it's worth the struggle.

But regardless of how imperfectly I live, and perhaps how ugly this part of the journey becomes, I only want to hear a few things. From my kids, "Daddy, I love you." "Daddy, thank you." From my wife, that the adventure has been better than she thought it could have been without me. Maybe, I'll even remember hearing it, for a few minutes.

So what will I do with the time I have, loose it or lose it. Time will tell.

And when I finish this earthly journey I will hear, "Well done, good and faithful servant."

AT THIS POINT

 May 7, 2014
Yet Another Blog

> Blogging - Never before have so many people with so little to say said so much to so few.[1]

So with that as an adequate introduction, here goes.

Frequency? Oh, that will be "periodically." I'm not a professional blogger, as will become evident very soon. I have a real job, one for the most part I enjoy. And like your job, it takes up space.

I admire those folks whose schedule, season of life, and discipline set the stage for them to post every week, at just about the same time every week. Or multiple times a week. Regimented. But that's not my schedule, my season of life, nor perhaps my discipline.

Consistency is difficult when a "random" week is consumed with a three-day retreat which is exactly my job and joy. Oh, and that's what's most important. That normal work is influenced by schedule, season of life, and discipline.

Will it be sarcastic at times? Absolutely. My name is James. Sarcasm—usually lightly humorous—is a normal part of life so of course it will find its way into my posts.

I've had stuff to say; some of it is even helpful.

Will I be misunderstood? Will I get myself in trouble? Yep. Why would this place in my world be any different? Oh, was that sarcasm?

And I have other priorities. I have kids at home I'm still trying to invest in wisely. Then there is this woman whom I want to remain

AT THIS POINT

married to. So—this blogging has some priority but its place isn't prominent.

For some of you, it will be difficult to believe that there have actually been some who have suggested I blog. Oh—and that they would read it. Go figure. So for those two or three people, here it is.

If it's helpful, tell me. If it's really helpful, tell someone else. If it's not that helpful, delete it and keep moving.

AT THIS POINT

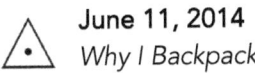
June 11, 2014
Why I Backpack

I've been asked from time to time why I backpack.

Last week my wife and I finished a 56.8 mile section of the Appalachian Trail (AT), a national scenic trail. We hiked four days with our friends Mike and Jessica who are thru-hiking the entire 2185.3 miles from Georgia to Maine. I'm fond of the AT, having hiked over 25% of the trail, multiple sections, multiple times. I have no idea how many miles I've backpacked.

I like to backpack, just not every step. It takes effort and some thought. What to take? What to do without? How far? How fast? Where will I sleep and in what? What will I eat?

But I get to live in simple beauty for a few days and see what some will never see: Mountain Laurel in huge shrubs, Fire Pink, a Scarlet Tanager, a black snake, the fog that's settled in a valley, rain coming down in sheets or a breath-taking vista like McAfee Knob.

I relish the joy of quiet miles to think, to pray, to sweat. I value unhurried conversation.

And while the troubles and disappointments of normal life follow me out into the woods, so does my life in Christ. It's that relationship which provides the foundation to sort through the rest of life.

On the trail, I have a cup. At home, I can choose from, well, too many cups.

At home, running water. Clean running water. I don't have to treat it or boil it. I can just enjoy it.

AT THIS POINT

I'm reminded and still get a little overwhelmed by the abundance I enjoy . . . and at times, hate . . . and at times, take for granted.

I'm reminded that so much of this world is geared toward creating discontentment. Sales papers. Ads. Newspaper articles. Facebook posts. Instagram. I'm reminded that the 24-hour news cycle does more harm than good.

I'm reminded that I can get caught up into someone else's agenda rather than living out life in Christ not compared to anyone else.

I'm reminded that I have more stuff than I really need. That my abundance can own me.

I'm reminded that the Body of Christ is so affected by the values of the world that it, too, seeks to amass temporal power and wealth . . . and so do I.

For you see, backpacking reminds me that I'm just a traveler here. I do not have as many days ahead of me as days behind me. Staying physically strong takes more work than it once did. Recovery takes longer too.

And I'm reminded that I'm not made just for this world.

I need those reminders.

Oh, what do I like about backpacking?

Stopping.

AT THIS POINT

 August 15, 2014
Steward

A couple of weeks ago my friend Kinley Winchester began his +/- thirty-hour trip to Erbil, Iraq, back to his family continuing to live out their life in Christ in the predominantly Islamic region of Kurdistan. They have lived there for three and a half of the last four years connected to the Classical School of the Medes and Servant Group International.

While he and his family are gone, I take care of their affairs on their behalf. In legal terms, I have durable power of attorney. So I'm their steward.

Although steward isn't used often in more recent Bible translations, it sticks in my mind as an important word. Being the Winchesters' steward isn't a huge deal and it's not tons of work. But being given this responsibility of a manager, administrator, gopher, grass mower, plumber, and helper has informed my ideas of being a steward of the resources placed in my care.

Here's what I'm thinking.

1. I lose identity.

I still remember one of the first bank deposits I made on their behalf. You know the process. Drive up to the window. Obligatory greetings. Deposit through the tube. Transaction complete. But then . . . "Can I help you with anything else Mr. Winchester?"

Mr. Winchester? That's not my name, but "they" think it is. I want to correct the teller because I know my name and I want people to know my name. In this case the bank teller doesn't know any differently. And it doesn't matter.

AT THIS POINT

I can get too concerned that people know my name and my work rather than the One whose business I represent.

2. I have this responsibility because I'm known.

Over the last 18 years Kinley and I have served together in multiple places from church to the Appalachian Trail and places in between. He knows me well. He knows my personality, my quirks, my fears, my inabilities, my heart.

Over these four years there have been a couple of memorable transactions that I haven't done so well. I dropped the ball. I didn't follow through. I failed. It cost them.

Are there other people who could have this responsibility? You betcha. Could they do it better than me? Most likely. Kinley knows me far better than most, yet he still trusts me.

So I have this stewardship not because I am more or less capable compared to anyone else. I have this stewardship because I am known.

3. Not my resources.

I can access accounts just like I do my own. I could sell their house if I wanted. I did sell their car (with their permission, of course).

I care for the house, communicate with potential and actual renters, make them aware of necessary decisions based on mail they receive. These resources that I have been asked to oversee are not mine to use how I want. While I can do what I want, I don't, because they're not my resources.

From time to time, I'm asked what I think or what I would do. I can freely give my opinion. And I have opinions. Some are helpful.

AT THIS POINT

When it comes right down to it, what matters most is what they want me to do, not what I want to do. Yep, there are obvious parallels to my relationship with Christ.

At this point, I want to be a good and faithful servant with the resources allowed to pass through my own fingers.

So what has God allowed to pass through your fingers, either of your own or someone else's? How are you doing at being a steward?

AT THIS POINT

 September 25, 2014
The Value of a Known Point

When I'm leading a small group team building session with a group of people who have been doing action-oriented, intense problem-solving activities, I may say, "Now we're going to do the hard part."

The looks I get make it seem like they're pretty sure they've just done the hard part.

And then I say, "We're going to think about what we've done. And since we're good Americans, we don't do that very often. We more often move from one thing to the next without giving much thought to where we are or where we came from or what we're doing."

I watch people's heads move up and down in agreement.

Delving into a recent challenging event can be helpful. Having a better idea of where we are at that known point can be a rich gift.

When using a map and compass for navigation, it's really helpful to know where you are before trying to get where you're going. If I know exactly where I am, then I really can better determine the direction in which I need to move.

And though it's really helpful to know where I am, sometimes I just kinda know where I am. And that's kinda helpful. Kinda knowing is far better than not knowing at all. In a world of unending, unexpected turns, maybe the best we can hope for is to kinda have an idea of where we are.

Life delivers rich gifts for us to learn where we are. If we don't pay attention, we'll miss it.

AT THIS POINT

Maybe our daily drive to work gives a clue, or the time taken to craft those 140 characters for all the world to see. Or the amount of time we spend watching YouTube videos or television or exploring the news. Maybe it's undesired loneliness or a relationship that's gone ugly and we're not quite sure why. What I gravitate to when it's too quiet or when I'm hurt or when I'm lonely or when I'm happy will give me an indication of where I am: that known point.

It might be the vocational, spiritual, intellectual, physical, familial, relational aspects of life or the overlapping influence of several. But when the circumstances of life pile up, and from that we get clarity, that is golden.

That known point could be a place of joy, of celebration, of gladness. It could be a place of fear, of doubt, of shame, of depression. Or maybe a point when I see more clearly my anger, my wavering self-worth, or the broken relationships of the past that affect the teetering relationships of the present.

We fear it will never change in this life. That we will never change in this life. That evil and haters and snippiness will overcome goodness. That God is not enough to be able to use this life affected by sin. That my relationships are just too messed up. That the events of the past will weigh me down and I'll crash into my own uselessness.

It's that gut check which reminds me how weak my faith is and how much I need to put my trust in God.

Perhaps hurt rises to the surface quickly. But that is telling too. And helpful. And not fun.

And as hard as these known points can be, they are gifts which I'm often slow to appreciate. In a world of unending unexpected

AT THIS POINT

turns, maybe the best we can hope for is to have sharp clarity for a fleeting moment. That place is holy. And hard, too.

But sometimes we just don't know where we are. And when you don't, what do you do? Take some time to pay attention to what's going on in your head and your heart right now. Step away from all the things that distract you and pay attention. Pay attention to what gets your attention.

A known point can be very helpful. A kinda known point can be helpful too. Instead of just moving to the next thing, there is great value in getting an idea of where we are.

What's going on in your world that is helping you to better know where you are? How do those current experiences help you determine where you are?

There is value in the known point.

AT THIS POINT

 November 11, 2014
Still in Tension

Just after daylight on a pleasant October morning in 1995, I stepped off with great anticipation and almost seventy miles ahead of me. My wife and nine-month-old son drove away. I was going to follow the painted blue turtle blazes of the Sheltowee Trace from Pickett State Park, Tennessee, to Cumberland Falls State Park, Kentucky. The goal was to backpack those 68.1 miles in three days or less.

A few kind people sponsored that hike to benefit the ministry I had founded, thus becoming the first "Backpack for BENCHMARK." I still have a few really clear mental snapshots of that trip. Some stories too.

The original plan was seventy miles of the Appalachian Trail in the Great Smoky Mountains National Park. Days before that 1995 hike, Hurricane Opal thrashed its way from Central America all the way to New England. In her entire path lay massive destruction; and the Smokies, including the Appalachian Trail, took a hit.

Only days before the start that original plan changed. Ain't that just like life?

I have twenty years of profound memories hoofing almost 600 miles of the Appalachian Trail, hiking multiple sections, multiple times, with more than fifty people on what we now call the "Chuck Wilson Memorial Backpack for BENCHMARK." Many of them have great memories too. And as you know, not only do plans change but time changes life too. This year during the Chuck Wilson, my once nine-month-old son was away at college while two high schoolers and a middle schooler were at home with a sitter.

AT THIS POINT

It wasn't long after that first Backpack for BENCHMARK before those 70 miles of the Appalachian Trail in the Smokies were back in my sights. Oh, I have fond memories of those first two hikes.

I made space to train. I valued the push and sweating, learning what my body was capable of doing. To have a body that can. To be privileged enough to have such an adventure as an option. By myself. On my schedule. I could hike as hard as I wanted at whatever pace my body and heart allowed. To stop and take in a view. To corral the emotions, the will, the body to move. To act. To be focused on a demanding goal and reaching it. It still makes me smile.

Adventures like those have helped me to see more clearly who I really am.

But after those two years, I was weary of working that hard and not sharing the journey with someone else.

What I missed was the shared experience. Shared joy. Shared discomfort. Shared accomplishment. Shared memories. And therein lies a tension between individual and group, private and public. This tension is a life tension.

Individual/Private <-------------------> Group/Public

If I am alone too much, that can become debilitating. Isolating. If I'm not alone enough, then those around me suffer. Both are good, in good measure.

There is much to be gained with focus on the individual/private (emotional, intellectual, spiritual, physical). There is also much to be gained with focus on the group/public (social, work, government).

AT THIS POINT

If I clamor for the group as my primary focus then I lose the intimacy of aloneness, the time for me to really see myself as I am. I need time to be quiet, to let my mind wander and settle. I can easily miss the nudge of the Spirit of God because I won't allow myself the space to hear.

What I know is that I'm responsible to God to live out my abilities and inabilities serving Christ for His Kingdom. I'm challenged to be a good and faithful servant. My overactive sense of responsibility has created problems at times. My heart has been questioned. My ideas were ignored.

I've watched many groups of students and adults stifle the great, bold ideas of an individual. Their own fear, insecurity, and pride didn't allow them to see the possibilities. They were much more comfortable with the least common denominator.

I get it. I've had some similar bold ideas. And I've stifled more than a few other people's ideas in the last twenty years.

While I have watched more than a minimal amount of television over the years, surfing the web and watching something else DVRed, it doesn't "test" me. It's OK to relax but my life shouldn't revolve around the next digital screen image.

Do I spend too much of life watching other people do stuff or am I doing, leading, and serving? Do I spend too much time doing and not enough time in quiet or developing those areas of private strength?

All the way back to Genesis, work was a part of life. So it's OK for my physical wellness to smack of work. Just about every health and wellness plan from back pain reduction, to Alzheimer's prevention, to depression alleviation, all have exercise or physical activity on the list. "Work" really is good for us—especially for those

AT THIS POINT

of us who work at a computer too much of the time. We need action.

If there aren't times when I get to test my physical capabilities, then I'm missing a real opportunity to see where I am–right now. The same can be said of other areas of life.

I can tell you, staying engaged as a husband and father with my family, my most intimate, immediate group, is much more of a challenge than backpacking 70 miles in three days or even 28 miles in a single day. Yet I often return a more settled man when I put in some hard miles. I had time to think, to dream, to pray, to just go.

I think I can still backpack that far. I think–I can.

At this point–I think I'll continue to wrestle with the tensions between individual responsibilities and the needs of the groups I'm involved in. That really is more difficult than seventy miles.

AT THIS POINT

 December 4, 2014
Keep Moving or Turn Back

A recent blast of cold has me thinking back to February 4, 2014.

The day started with the Center for Nonprofit Management's first morning workshop, "Effectively Managing Your Time." The rest of the day felt like I hadn't learned a thing as I moved from one thing to the next.

The more regular work moved right into an evening Board of Directors meeting with planning for the second annual ministry celebration; details, details, details; and passionate conversation about how to restate more clearly the mission of BENCHMARK. By the time it was over I needed to work over my thoughts. Life had squeezed out my training run earlier and I needed to get it in before bed.

Back home. It's 9:30 p.m. Dark. But I've run in the dark before. It's cold, upper 30s. But I've run in the cold before. It's raining and has been for hours. But I've been wet before, so out the door I go.

It's a familiar route: out Nebraska Avenue, jump on the greenway to go around the back side of McCabe golf course, cross the Richland Creek bridge, behind the U.S. Army Reserve center, cross another bridge, up by the railroad tracks to Cherokee Avenue to Westlawn Drive and home. Four miles.

Did I mention it had been raining? The day's total was shaping up for two inches.

So off I go. Around McCabe golf course, I find some standing water on the greenway. That's not unusual when it's been raining, but now my feet are getting wet and my toes are starting to get cold. Upper 30s, remember?

AT THIS POINT

Not much further and Richland Creek is clearly out of its banks, now completely covering the greenway. Oh, this ain't good. It's now over my shoes and I have completely wet feet. Again, not my first time, but I could feel the cold moving up my legs.

For at least 200 feet I splash my way through shin deep water, high stepping it all the way. As I approach a little rise in the greenway I'm trying to decide whether to keep moving or turn back. My mind is racing. What's the risk? What if I go down and then get fully soaked? Did I tell my wife my route? This skinny body doesn't like to go "all in" cold water in cold weather.

Though I know this route, I don't know it quite so well underwater, water splashing up above my knees, in that temperature. I know what's behind me and not sure of what's ahead of me. Keep moving or turn back?

I've bumped into life hard enough to ask myself that question more than a few times. Haven't you?

This nonprofit I've led for twenty-one years called BENCHMARK Adventure Ministries—keep moving or turn back?

I taught college for seven years and there were not a few times when I would ask—keep moving or turn back?

What about stepping off a 180' rappel? Or reaching for that next awkward climbing hold that's going to stretch me, and my belayer, a little further than I wanted to be stretched? Or hitting whitewater in an open canoe with the skills I have?

How about investing deeply in a local church? That relationship with a coworker or friend that turned ugly? Perhaps the pressured submission from poor leadership that too highly values wide-ranging compliance?

Even more consequential: what about marriage and parenting?

AT THIS POINT

I feel it in my chest and in my throat. Sometimes in my arms. That uneasy feeling that things are changing and may do so remarkably.

You and I have both lived long enough to ask the keep moving or turn back question in one way or the other. My tendency is to splash right on in and to keep going until I'm stopped. It has served me well. Most of the time.

And I've stayed put when others left and made an eternal impact.

I've also lived long enough to realize there have been times when I should have turned back but I stuck it out and created more problems for everyone, and myself.

But what about you? What are you shin deep in right now that has you wondering if you should keep going or turn back? It's that place where fear and uncertainty creeps in and you're put through it.

You may get through it and find out, in time, that you were stretched beyond your ability to endure and came out stronger, or deeper, or kinder, or steadier, or more joyful, or seeing your life more clearly as a vapor, or with a fresh ability to see someone else's perspective.

Or, you may look back on it with deep hurt and wish you had chosen differently.

So I finished that run. Feet, legs, and belly red from the cold. Thankful that I didn't go down. Wondering if I had leveraged the grace of God foolishly. Realizing I'd pushed through something hard. Again.

Oh, for the wisdom of God and an obedient heart to be more responsive in the middle of fear, hesitation, uncertainty, hurt, and fuzzy understanding.

AT THIS POINT

I'm very clear there has been a time or two when I was ready to stop and just walk away, when I was ready to quit, but I'm still here.

At this point—I think I'll just keep moving and see where this journey takes me.

AT THIS POINT

 December 18, 2014
Immanuel With Us

> Therefore the Lord himself will give you a sign:
> The virgin will conceive and give birth to a son,
> and will call him Immanuel. (Isaiah 7:14)

> The virgin will conceive and give birth to a son,
> and they will call him Immanuel. (Matthew 1:23)

Recently in a church round table discussion we were asked to share our favorite Christmas tradition. Most around the table were much more thoughtful than me. I had my mind on the purpose of the informational meeting and those people sitting at my table. And not much further.

I don't always think well on my feet.

I gave some yammering, lame response about watching It's A Wonderful Life and the time on Christmas day to just unhurriedly mess around with some home project since it's our family of six around on Christmas day.

With some thought afterwards, it could have been . . .

- the bright white and gold porcelain nativity figures that I bought for Barbara a few years ago that decorate our living room. There's another nativity outside.
- a "live" Christmas tree that's cut and dying with ornaments stretching from my childhood to last year's addition. One year we bought a live, balled and burlapped tree. It died too. So we now go straight for the

AT THIS POINT

tree we know is dead instead of waiting for the slower, same outcome.
- watching the kids go right to playing with or using some gift they've been given.

With additional reflection, I'm reminded it's not a tradition that's my favorite Christmas tradition. At this time of year, for me it's Immanuel.

That simple word, that name, carries so much weight. God became man. The Creator became the created. It's profound. Immanuel, which means . . . God with us.

God with us is different from God for us. I get caught up in for and against.

While I sincerely believe that God is not against me, He is also not for my preferences, my pet projects. In our society driven by rabid competition we think in terms of for/against. He is not for my political preference, my race, my nationality, my favorite sports team, the city I live in, my favorite nonprofit, the local church I attend and against someone else's.

God can be with people who have diametrically opposite views. His being with me supersedes simple tolerance, which is a high value in our culture . . . maybe even worshiped. It's not "for/against" as in "win/lose."

He is for His own glory, for His character, for His purposes. He desires for us to be aligned with that.

And He knows we're all a little bit off.

He made creation so that we could know Him. He wants us to know Him. God did tell us some stuff . . . some important stuff . . . all pointing toward His coming, His presence, His being near. God with us.

AT THIS POINT

When I hit a hard spot in life, it's comforting and appreciated when someone is for me. Being for me it is far better than ignoring me. But when I check in on my emotional needs, it's better when just the right person is with me. "With me" is personal.

Presence is more substantial than assent or appreciation.

He is not for the fear, hurt, depression, discouragement. That is not God's desire for me. But when I am fearful, hurt, depressed or discouraged, He is with me. He wants me to live life with Him.

And He is, through His Spirit, still with us. I didn't run Him off like a former friend. I haven't offended Him. He hasn't fired me. He didn't vote me off the island. He wants His best for me. And even though I can walk away from Him, He is still with me . . . with us. God has sent His Son to model how we should respond. Being with is more personal; it means being near.

God with us moves me to live with people; to imperfectly embody the perfect Son He sent, to desire more deeply the presence of God and to live out that presence. God with us, that idea, that reality, informs my life of ministry. And truth be told, it's the reality of God with us that I want to affect all of my days.

I can tell people stuff and it may be helpful. If I am with them it may be better. When God is with us, it is better.

Yes, God is slowly but surely being written out of the script of life; culturally, politically, socially, and even religiously; yet, He still is with us. He is near. He is here.

At this point, I'll focus my attention on the profound reality of Immanuel, God with us.

AT THIS POINT

 December 25, 2014
A Post-Christmas Prayer

On the cusp of our Christmas celebration, will you oh God, make yourself known in the middle of violence, anger, injustice, military involvement, corporate misdealings, political messes, materialism and narcissism, just as you did when Christ came. Quietly. Purposefully. At just the right time.

Would you do something else amazing and help people to see Christ in me, in spite of my own self-righteousness?

Help me to compare my righteousness and love to yours so that I more clearly see how much I need you.

AT THIS POINT

 April 5, 2015
Happy Easter. He's Alive.

But please allow me to digress for a few minutes.

I needed a haircut this week. And it wasn't because Easter is approaching and I need to look good on stage. The two men ahead of me at the barbershop did want haircuts for that reason, and it's a good enough reason to get a haircut. But I'll not be on stage anywhere.

After letting my hair grow out as much as I would allow for my ten-day ministry trip in the north Georgia woods to gain me as much insulation on my head as my head could grow, I was back home, and it was time for a haircut.

Patti is my barber who has cut my hair for over ten years. She is a self-described "formerly Catholic, probably Buddhist" with roots in San Diego. She and I are very different, and we've had some very interesting conversations over the years.

She remembers I taught at a Bible college and that I'm currently in ministry. She'll ask me religious questions from time to time but also about what I've been doing.

After listening to her conversations with the first two men about their Easter involvement, I chuckled and said to her something like, "It may be worth paying attention to, Patti, that the first three people in your chair this morning are heading toward Easter." She laughed and deflected.

When I sat in the chair, I told her about spending ten days serving hikers on the Appalachian Trail passing out apples, preparing food, and making available waterproof portions of the New Testament to hikers. She asked if the hikers had to pay. "Of course not."

AT THIS POINT

"Apples?" Patti, like others, went there. "Wasn't that what Eve ate . . . an apple?"

I laughed, "Well we don't know for sure. The Bible doesn't say apple, tradition does. The Bible says fruit. But we don't know if it was an apple. It's important to pay attention to what the Bible actually says. Kinda like Jonah and the whale; the Bible says big fish."

So off that conversation went, ending with "You don't believe that, do you, that Jonah was swallowed by a whale?"

My nudge was to look at what the Bible says, not at what we're told about what the Bible says.

A friend of hers came in with an Easter basket for her. Patti drew him into the conversation by asking him, a former Southern Baptist, if he thought Jonah was swallowed by a whale. He did not but was so very kind in not wanting to hamper anyone's belief if they did. I affirmed that I was that kind of believer.

The conversation then went to hunting Easter eggs (connected to the Easter bunny), Easter Sunday, and the potential confusion it can create since only one is true, that it's for the children and that we still hunt Easter eggs at our house, to "oh, you have children."

During the conversation I said what I say from time to time: "Children are part of the reason why I need Jesus."

Patti says, "Oh, I bet you are a great father, a fun father".

"But you should ask my kids. I need Jesus."

That's why the Resurrection is so very important. I need Jesus. In my clearest reflections on life, I have a sense of how selfish and self-righteous I am.

AT THIS POINT

> In today's world, we are prone to viewing ourselves primarily as righteous people who are capable of doing sinful things, as opposed to being sinful people who are capable of doing righteous things. The difference in perspective is monumental. – James Bryan Smith, Embracing the Love of God[1]

I am not a righteous person who occasionally does sinful things; I am a sinful person who occasionally does good.

And so, as I step into Easter, it's not about getting a haircut or being on stage or church traditions or misunderstandings about what the Bible says. It's not about Easter eggs, certainly not the Easter bunny or apples or new clothes.

Easter is about being really sure that I need Jesus.

I'm so grateful He is alive.

At this point, I want to live in freedom in that truth.

AT THIS POINT

 April 19, 2015
No Telling Who I'll Bump Into

I plan to run another marathon this Saturday.

Last year was my fifteenth Country Music Marathon here in Nashville, Tennessee. It's the only marathon I've run and I am one of about forty people who have run all fifteen. Only about sixteen people have run the full race each year.

As my fellow fifteen-year runner and sixteenth-year registrant Larry Epps puts it, "I sometimes think I'm just too stupid to stop."

This annual run has been a point of evaluation for me. It gives me a chance to think about how fortunate I've been to be healthy enough to run fifteen of these things. It reminds me of what I've lived through. It reminds me that continued health is this unequal tension between my part: sleep, care for this temporal body, eat well, and train; and God's part, His abundant grace.

I've been thinking about last year's run for a year. On Saturday's long training run for this marathon, I was thinking about my best memory from last year.

I had such hopes for the fifteenth marathon, but about Mile 22, the weather was taking its toll on me as it headed toward a high of eighty-three degrees. The gaps in training from ministry travel and "just life" were making themselves very evident. By Mile 24, I was coming out of Shelby Park with heavy feet. My hope of a reasonably good time for me had faded. I call Shelby Park the place where marathon dreams go to die. I just didn't have the stamina or mental depth to maintain my pace. But I was still moving.

From my perspective, if it's a great day for spectators, it's not a good day to run a marathon. If it's a little chilly and rainy for

AT THIS POINT

spectators, then it's a good day for me to run. My fifteenth marathon was a great day for spectators.

After getting worked over by a final, small hill at 5th and Shelby about a half mile from the finish line—where I had walked some, again—I turned left onto Woodland Street for the final downhill to LP Field. I was whipped but moving well.

There I saw a young man walking. Based on his shirt and haircut I said, "Where we going Soldier?" He looked out of the corner of his eye.

It was one of those looks that communicates, "Oh man, that's an old guy and he said what?"

So I added, "Let's go, sir."

I call every Soldier sir.

I ran the last half mile with that young Soldier who I learned was from Fort Campbell. Just a little while before that, I had been walking.

I thanked him for serving and that his service helps to make it possible for me to run fifteen Country Music Marathons in freedom. The emotion was building in me.

Nearing the final turn to the finish line I pointed to my kids who were yelling my name and told him his work helps to keep them safe.

I was overcome by emotion. Finishing a marathon is emotional for me. It's done.

After we finished, he said to me, "You kicked my ass, sir, or I'd still be walking." I shook his hand and thanked him for running with an old guy. I'm sure I didn't kick his ass. An old guy just nudged him along. And I needed someone to run with. It was one of the highlights of the day.

AT THIS POINT

We got into the finishers area and I shouted, "Here's a currently serving military man!"

As someone approached, the young Soldier said again, "And he kicked my ass."

Truth is, it was a joy to run with him to the finish line. It helped to adjust my perspective. I run in freedom because other people stand on the wall and God has been so very gracious to this country.

My sixteenth Country Music Marathon is this Saturday, April 25th. My wife Barbara, who has run thirteen Country Music Marathons, and I will gather with 25,000 of our closest friends on Broadway in downtown Nashville to run.

Run . . . because we can.

At this point, I'll do my part to keep this aging body moving. I'll eat as well as I can. I'll make sleep a priority. I'll manage my emotional and intellectual capabilities and inabilities as well as I am able, submitted to God.

I run, not as an end in itself. I want to be fit to serve in Christ's name. I want to keep up with my kids. I want to be able to say to others, "Let's go," rather than, "You go ahead."

And there is no telling who I'll bump into.

AT THIS POINT

 May 14, 2015
Still Learning from Doing

Much of my life of ministry revolves around learning from doing. It's something I'm practicing and still learning. More and more I understand how important it is. Doing and then learning from it is critical to growth. It's the idea of action/reflection.

I've done some things but didn't learn lessons well. I would have benefited from learning. I just went on to the next thing. Haven't you?

Recently, I completed my sixteenth Country Music Marathon. The 26.2 mile course is a culmination of sixteen weeks of training, focus, and to some degree figuring out what to say yes to and what to say no to. Saying yes to running is a plus.

This year the field for the 2015 Country Music Marathon was over 27,000 runners; most ran the 13.1 mile half marathon. Less than 10% of all runners completed the full marathon. I'm one of about thirty-eight people who have run all sixteen Country Music full or half marathons. About twelve to fourteen people have run all sixteen full marathons. I'm persistent, just not fast.

The hope on the day of a marathon is that all the pieces will come together: training, emotional resilience, physical stamina, sleep, food, water, and weather.

After running sixteen of these, it normally doesn't just come together.

A younger running friend of mine texted me after she finished. "That's it, James. You are certifiably crazy. Anyone who can run sixteen of these blasted things is nuts! I am teasing you, btw. I am disappointed I didn't see you guys. I hope you had a good run

AT THIS POINT

today. Thankfully the pesky lightning held off, but those last miles were humid!"

Marathons are a wonderful metaphor for life. It's about overcoming. Pushing on. Attempting a challenge that few take on and few get to do.

Over these sixteen years, I've stepped to the starting line:
- after getting fired mid-semester from a seven-year college teaching position,
- after not being able to run for two months because I broke a rib one January,
- with a bulging disk in my lower back. I could hardly get out of bed and I couldn't sit very long, but it turns out I could still run.

Fortunately, not all those things happened the same year.

This year, even with a two-week gap in my critical March training due to ministry travel and BENCHMARK's Appalachian Trail Outreach, I woke with anticipation. I recently wrote in a post, "If it's a great day for spectators, it's not a good day to run a marathon. If it's a little chilly and rainy for spectators . . . it's a good day to run."

The day was shaping up to be a great day for spectators.

After crowded roads and a slower start in the first three miles I was back on pace. Through Music Row, Belmont Boulevard, the Gulch, out and back into Metro Center, through downtown, past LP Field, and up the long steady hill of Woodland Street, past Five Points in East Nashville for the first eighteen miles, my pace was good but taxing. Then I walked about a block. Getting back on pace, the sun came out about mile 21. With five miles to go I thought a personal best was in my sights.

AT THIS POINT

As I was heading out of Shelby Park, I saw U.S. Army Chaplain (CPT) Kevin Trimble just entering Shelby Park. BENCHMARK Adventure Ministries supported a retreat he led in Kansas, the 7th Chaplains Partnership Initiative ministry event. I knew he ran but didn't expect to see him in Nashville. He was having a conversation with someone so I greeted him and eased ahead.

By mile 23, the wheels were coming off. A personal best was slipping away. My legs didn't want to move and I wasn't sure I cared if they did. By mile 24 I wasn't able to muster the courage to get my body moving very fast. When a body slows down "after a marathon" it begins to function again. And since I had been walking, my body and my mind thought I was done. I was getting concerned that my body was going to rebel. I wasn't happy about that.

By mile 25 the wheels were off and I wasn't sure I was going to finish or even wanted to.

Yep, with a little over a half mile to go and very close to the same spot where I ran up behind a Soldier last year, I sat down on the curb.

The mental and emotional strain of the last two weeks followed me onto the course. I couldn't outrun it and hadn't worked through it.

I sat for two or three minutes . . . thinking . . . talking to myself. I'd already been talking to myself over the previous two miles and it hadn't been helpful. It's not my normal to quit, to stop, to not go on when it gets tough. But it was reality on that day.

Overall my training had gone well and my times were consistently stronger than recent years. I had thought a hamstring issue was going to be my Achilles heel.

AT THIS POINT

I stood up. I may have taken a step or two and then I heard, "I can't think of anyone else I would like to finish the race with." It was Chaplain Trimble. He talked me into running again. He told me to "run harder" and "give it all you got." I took another break with hands on my knees underneath the I-65 overpass on Woodland Street. I thought a banana I had eaten in Shelby Park was going to come back up. With some encouragement, I finished. Chaplain Trimble and I had a picture taken together.

I finished my sixteenth full marathon and I'm about "average," about in the middle, of my sixteen marathon finish times, the overall marathon finish times, my age group division and gender. Average will have to do. Healthy enough to be average is a gracious gift of God.

Encouragement is so vital. I don't do it well. I facilitate experiences with people drawing out the obvious and oft-hidden gems of life from those experiences.

For much of my life, I've not needed much encouragement. In the day to day, I don't encourage well.

At this point, I need to be more liberal with encouragement; pointed, specific, timely encouragement for others to keep going and to run their daily race of life as well as they can run it. . . in Christ.

And when the wheels start coming off, maybe, just maybe, someone will come along to run a few steps with you.

AT THIS POINT

August 19, 2015
Best Trail Magic

On the second day of our five-day family backpacking trip in Virginia, we sat by beautiful Fox Creek sharing lunch with a middle-aged female thru-hiker who was hiking by herself with support from her husband. As usual, I packed too much for lunch and snacks.

(Yes, it is possible to have too much to eat on a backpacking trip.)

She was a pleasant woman who talked about how great it was that the entire family, all six of us, were backpacking together. She was planning to hike the entire 2180 miles of the Appalachian Trail in about six months. We were planning to backpack a 55.7-mile section. And since we were a little heavy with lunch leftovers, we were happy to share them with her, and told her so. She was more willing to eat our food since we had "extra." The Evans herd had completed almost twelve miles the first day and were enough into Day 2 that food was optimal. After sharing stories, our lunch, and the spot by Fox Creek, it was time for us to head our separate directions, her to the north, us toward the south.

We left the creek and crossed a road where we recognized familiar faces. "Twixless" and "Whisper," (trail names, since most thru-hikers don't use their real names on the AT) were a brother and sister whom we had served on BENCHMARK's Appalachian Trail Outreach in March. When we met them in Georgia they had completed about seventeen miles. Twelve weeks later they had completed 508 miles. Sitting by a paved road, they didn't know how much in the middle of nowhere they were but were getting

AT THIS POINT

ready to hitchhike to the nearest town because they were out of food.

"We have some extra," I offered. It saved them some miles, lightened our load, and filled their bellies. After a brief conversation we were off. They were smiling. So were we.

Before the trip, we had wondered if we would see any of over 500 people to whom we gave apples, shared camp, with and served in BENCHMARK's "popup cafe." I didn't expect to see anyone, thinking that the hiker "bubble" would be further north than where we were hiking. But I was wrong.

Up and across the marvelous Virginia and Grayson Highlands washed in great views, great weather, and of course, "wild" ponies, we were gathering great memories together. After leaving the Grayson Highlands and the Mount Rogers area, we were heading down a long slow decline. Heading up the trail came a married couple we remembered from Georgia. He is a larger, gruff man with a full black beard and thick Northern accent. He and his petite wife were steadily hiking that very long hill. They were from "New"—New York or New Jersey. They, too, recognized us or at least they said they did. We chatted for a couple of minutes and off they went. Three months of their journey put them completing about 495 miles. That's lots of miles done, but even more yet to go. They were "behind" but still moving.

As we continued down the trail I asked my wife, "Do you honestly think it really makes a difference? Do you think people really remember us and what we do on the Appalachian Trail Outreach?"

Not far down the trail the Evans herd stopped for a potty break and another lunch. We heard the voices of a young couple who were moving along pretty well. We recognized them. We thought

AT THIS POINT

they recognized some of us. It had been three months. We asked about their hike. By that point, most thru-hikers should be around the 1000-mile mark. "Wing Nut" and "Foxy" happily chatted about the days since we last saw them. They had left the trail for some time to recover from knee problems, spending some time beach hopping. That time off the trail had hampered their long-distance hiking progress. But then their memories, without help, got better.

"Oh man, yours was the best trail magic," they told us. "That big shelter. The food. Those Dutch oven desserts, that was the best. We compare everybody else to your trail magic because it was so good." We signed Wing Nut's backpack and off we all went with smiles on our faces.

There you have it, some do still remember, even three months later. We had made an impression. In Christ's name, we hope.

We hope everyone we have served will remember the great food, the wonderful Dutch oven desserts, the kind service, the clean conversation, the willingness to help. Most of all, we hope they remember that the reason we serve them is because we have been served. We share before each main meal that it is our relationship with Christ, His service to us, that compels us to serve.

We serve not because we must, but because we get to.

I have served poorly. We all sometimes miss the mark. There are times when service is not well received. Perhaps I serve others the way I want to serve instead of how they need to be served. I still miss at times, and that's just in my own home. But I'm still trying. From time to time, I serve well. It's meaningful for servant and receiver. It makes us both smile.

Though there are times when I think I am done, at this point, I'll try to learn from the times I have served poorly, celebrate God's

AT THIS POINT

good work in and through me when I serve well, and leave God with the results. There is no guarantee that it will change the world. But it may feed some memories that God can use to change a life.

AT THIS POINT

 March 6, 2016
Layering

In the first two months of 2016, I've talked to three distinctly different groups about layering: a Boy Scout troop, 4:13 Strong, and Men of Valor.

Spending some time in the backcountry over many years, I've practiced layering and have landed on some things that work for me, in most weather conditions, based on my body type. It's certainly not one-size fits all.

Layering is selecting layers of clothing and using them in a functional combination to care for yourself. That way, you can care for others and make the most of the time in the backcountry or work in a harsh climate.

I've heard it said, "There is no bad weather, just bad clothing choices."

So I have a system, a simple set of cards that I created in the early 1990's that I still use when I pack every trip. These "trip cards" are 3x5 index cards cut in half. On each card is an item that I may need or a group of similar items from which I can select for the particular trip. Clothing for twenty degrees is different than what I need for ninety degrees. By the time I work through each card, the items I need are all gathered. This simple system keeps me from overpacking, and ensures I have what I may need.

Rather than rethinking my actual "trip cards," I've been thinking about the principles behind these kinds of lists recently and their implications to life.

1. Take off/Put on: - put on character, take off . . .
We all put things on we shouldn't: habits, sin, anger, bitterness,

AT THIS POINT

weight.

A number of years ago I put on fifteen pounds. It was weight I didn't need nor want and it was time for it to go. I realized that it had taken about nine months to put that weight on and I was going to give myself about nine months to get it off. I gave myself some grace.

Do you see what I did to myself there? I ratcheted down the pressure. So many times I've created unnecessary pressure for myself to achieve something.

2. Do with what you have until you can do different.

Doing with what I have is an exercise in contentment. That whole "I can do all things through Christ who gives me strength" is the conversation from Philippians 4 on contentment, not a physical challenge.

I have an L.L. Bean fleece that my wife bought for me five or six years ago from Goodwill for $5. The retail price was about $65. I've worn it all over the place in all kinds of conditions. It has served me well but it also looks pretty rough now.

For Christmas, I was on the search for another jacket to keep me warm and take me into the future. With advice, I landed on a Mountain Hardwear Compressor. It's a well-built, outdoor grade jacket and I found a last year's model for half price. It's most certainly a step up from a fleece.

As I write, I'm wearing the fleece because I was in a muddy cave earlier today. I'll switch to the warmer Mountain Hardwear jacket as the sun goes down and the temperature drops.

I enjoyed the fleece and wore it out. I was content with it. I'm enjoying the new jacket because it's new and because it's much warmer than the fleece.

AT THIS POINT

I learned to do with what I had and learned to be content with what I had, until I needed to and could do different.

3. Everything weighs something.

On the long wilderness trips I led during the 1990s and on backpacking trips with newer hikers, we do a pack shakedown. It's when a more experienced hiker reviews every item a less experienced hiker plans to take, for the purpose of reducing weight.

On the monster canopy in our Appalachian Trail Outreach campsite hangs a sign: "Pack Shake Down? Ask James."

When someone asks for a pack shakedown, they likely already think they are carrying too much. It begins with "Get everything out of your pack you want me to see."

There are three rules to remember:

Rule #1: This is your stuff. You brought it here and you can leave with everything you brought.

Rule #2: I'll tell you what I think. But, refer to Rule #1, it's your stuff. You brought it here and you can leave with everything you brought.

Rule #3: Everything weighs something.

Those are very practical guidelines.

They are coming for food. They don't care who we are. But they also don't know who we are.

4. Appearance is not nearly as important as our culture communicates.

Our culture worships appearance just like every other culture on the planet has done. Form vs Function. Pretty people, pretty colors, pretty places. I like those things too.

AT THIS POINT

For the outdoors, function is much more important.

So, take off and put on what will help you on your journey. Continue to learn to be content. Appearance is not nearly as important as our culture communicates.

AT THIS POINT

 November 11, 2016
I Remember You

> "I thank my God every time I remember you. In all my prayers for all of you, I always pray with joy because of your partnership in the gospel from the first day until now, being confident of this, that he who began a good work in you will carry it on to completion until the day of Christ Jesus." (Philippians 1:3-6)

For twenty-two months I've almost exclusively read and listened to Paul's letter to the Philippians found in the Bible. Its four brief chapters have pointed instruction mixed with such a hopeful, future tone. I have no idea how many times I've been through this letter to date but I keep going back to it. This morning, yet again, I was struck.

Paul remembers.

Remembering can be healthy. Some call it reflection. As he sat incarcerated in Rome for being a follower of Jesus Christ, he was reminded of those believers in the city of Philippi who had been in partnership with him since the beginning.

The people who knew Paul also knew about his past—a history of persecuting Christians before he became one—yet they stuck with him anyway. It seems reasonable they partnered with Paul because he was about more than himself. They saw something in him. He was about the Gospel.

And perhaps too, their hope for Paul was the same as he expressed for them, "that he who began a good work in you will carry it on to completion" (Philippians 1:6).

AT THIS POINT

Paul believed the death, burial, and resurrection of Jesus Christ was true and the reality of that belief was being worked out in his own life. It shaped him and his priorities.

We're about 2000 years post Paul's earthly life. I haven't known the Gospel from the beginning, but Paul did. Because of Paul and a whole host of other imperfect followers of Jesus Christ, I too believe. I too want the Gospel to affect every part of my imperfect life. And mirroring verse 27 of the first chapter, I want to conduct myself in a manner worthy of the gospel of Christ, whatever happens.

In a conversation at our headquarters earlier this week, a staff member asked what I wanted for those who are involved with BENCHMARK. Philippians does a great job of defining that hope.

I want to be aligned with God's best interest for you. I want He who began a good work in you to carry it out to completion, wherever in the Kingdom you are led to serve.

Being involved with an organization for over twenty-three years, I have a ton of memories. I remember people who were instrumental in helping BENCHMARK get started. I remember others who have been a part of my life for a season and some for long stretches. I remember my parents who always encouraged me to follow Christ, no matter what. I remember people who have come and gone. I remember those still around.

People have donated, prayed and encouraged God's good work in me so that life will be much less about me and much more about life in Christ which has been their hope for me and my hope for others.

There are times when I've been a little sore about those who have come and gone. But in my best mind, when I am thinking

AT THIS POINT

well, I trust that God manages His Kingdom and His servants well. I trust that He is working in my best interest and in theirs.

And I pray with joy. I pray for those who were and are currently involved in my life and the ministry I lead. It's the always part of praying where I need to be more consistent.

At this point, I remember you.

AT THIS POINT

 March 7, 2017
Cannot Be Explained Medically

Not many people know, but a BENCHMARK champion collapsed from a heart attack on February 15, 2017, while on training run for his first marathon in the United States.

First of all, for those on BENCHMARK's Prayer Team who have been praying, thank you. Really, thank you.

Second, I've been slow to send this update because I've been trying to catch up on my immediate work and trying to let my head and heart catch up to where my body is.

Kinley Winchester has been my friend for twenty years. He is a healthy, strong man. A Christ honoring man. He and his family served in Erbil, Iraq, for four and a half years teaching in a Kurdish school and sharing their lives with the Muslim community. They returned to the States about a year and a half ago.

After his heart attack, he had a stent implanted and was placed in a medically induced coma. His body was cooled below ninety degrees for his brain to rest. Though there were promising initial signals (eye flutter, gag reflex, and he was breathing on his own when brought in), there was no assurance of his outcome and we would have to wait as the professionals worked their medical protocols.

About 165 hours, just a few hours shy of exactly a week after he collapsed, Kinley returned home. He walked on his own, in his right mind with very minor short-term memory loss. Within two days, he took a two mile walk around a lake.

Oh, I could go on and on about ways God has shown off. Yes, there was a great doctor who did an emergency procedure and a wonderful, attentive nursing staff. But what has happened with my

AT THIS POINT

friend "cannot be explained medically," his doctor said. The nurses have said "amazing," "wonderful, "night and day difference," "miracle." His sister calls him Lazarus. The cardiologist doesn't have a category for Kinley's inexplicable recovery. Perhaps his patient will be part of God drawing a cardiologist to Himself.

I sat in my friend's room after he came out of coma and listened to his wife talking with Muslim friends in Kurdistan who were concerned about their friend as well. God has and is making Himself known through the friendships they developed internationally and their testimony through this heart attack. I was delighted to listen and celebrate with them.

At this point, I'm incredibly grateful for God's gracious answer to the faithful prayers of so many people who love Kinley and his family.

AT THIS POINT

 February 17, 2018
Start Again

> The steadfast love of the Lord never ceases; his mercies never come to an end; they are new every morning; great is your faithfulness. (Lamentations 3:22-23 ESV)

December is time for personal evaluation. January is for fresh implementation. I'm not much for New Year's resolutions. I prefer regular evaluation and direction correction.

January 2018 started well with a renewed commitment to personal, spiritual journaling. I began training for my nineteenth 26.2-mile marathon. Though I've been reading Philippians for years, I added one chapter in Proverbs a day. It's that idea of reading the Proverb that corresponds to the day of the month. Both books have wisdom I need.

I committed to donors and those interested in the ministry I lead that I would be more consistent in communication. It's been an ongoing challenge to do the tasks that need to be done and to communicate well.

Preparation was made for BENCHMARK's Leadership Development Retreat and our twentieth year to serve Brentwood United Methodist sixth graders with twelve staff members coming together for two days. Icy Nashville weather brought that opportunity and that twenty-year streak to an end. It was preparation without execution.

On January 16th I left for my hometown in South Georgia to address family business for my mama. I pushed long days trying to get done all I could as quickly as I could. I woke on Sunday the

AT THIS POINT

21st not feeling well and chose to rest. Monday I was back working hard.

By Tuesday night I was not in good shape and heading back to Tennessee.

For over two weeks I cycled between the bed, couch, floor, and dining room table. Whatever I had developed into bronchitis.

I wrote in my journal: "I've been sick so long I watched the Fate of the Furious yesterday afternoon."

If you don't know, it's the eighth Fast and Furious movie. I now know why I haven't watched the other seven. But I was sick, so cut me some slack. Please.

My two plus weeks being down halted early January's progress.

You get it. Life happens. What to do?

Start again!

As I could, I focused on the important and urgent: reports for the National Forest Service and Mission Increase Foundation, donor receipts, accounting reconciliation, and the 120+ pages of a general liability renewal application. I needed to figure out what I dropped so I could pick it back up.

As I could, I focused on the important and not urgent; running miles again, slowly, reading Proverbs, journaling, work, and family relationships.

Lying on the couch for two weeks interrupted my decision not to watch the national or local news early in the day. Life is better when I don't. So, as best as I could, I started again.

Reflecting on the Good News is a better start than the news. Something as simple as,

"Thank you Lord, I'm alive."

"I choose to live today in Christ."

"God help us."

AT THIS POINT

So what about you? Did January squeeze out your New Year's resolution? Evaluate those previous decisions. Keep some. Throw out others. Adjust. Start again.

Maybe you watch TV or stare at your mobile device too much. I have. Do it less. That's always a good call.

Is it a moral failure? Repent. Turn from it. Walk in grace. Live out the consequences. Start again in a new direction.

Small incremental changes make a huge difference over time. Start again doing what you know is good, healthy, and life-giving for yourself and others. Go back to the gym. Take that walk. Read a chapter in that book or The Book. Move toward the faithfulness of God. You'll be more aware of your lack of faithfulness and His great faithfulness.

At this point, I'm trying to focus on what's important, whether urgent or not urgent. I'm still trying to catch up doing what I needed to be doing and trying to be patient as I recover. I am only responsible to live the life I've been given.

This morning, I start again.

Will you join me?

AT THIS POINT

 March 15, 2018
Frustrating People for 25 Years

I find myself a little overwhelmed.

On March 15, 1993, "it" began. When "it" started, "it" didn't have a name. Over the next year a name was determined, corporation papers submitted, excess medical coverage for participants obtained, nonprofit status applied for and gained.

My mind is racing through so many people who were instrumental in the early years of BENCHMARK Adventure Ministries. I think of Mark McPeak, who was the adult pastor of the church I attended at the time, who encouraged the gifts he saw in me and used his own considerable gifts to move BENCHMARK forward. It was Mark who wrote BENCHMARK's appeal letter for our very first Backpack for BENCHMARK in 1995 and fifty people donated.

I think of Vicky Smith and my wife Barbara who for years encouraged me, and along with Mark McPeak became BENCHMARK's Advisory Board in early 1994. Later that year Jim Lauthern joined us. They served a lot of years and I am grateful. I could list the other eighteen men and women who have served on the Board over the years. It'd be a longer list of the instructors who have been a part of our staff or those hundreds of organizational leaders who invited BENCHMARK to be a part of their ongoing ministries.

We've served over 13,000 participants through 434 ministry events, so it would read like one of those Biblical genealogies and you'd stop reading. But just like a seemingly boring genealogy, there is richness and depth in God's grace that's worth acknowledging.

AT THIS POINT

Our interactive experiences and outdoor adventures create a setting for all involved to consider how they're currently living with an eye toward being different, better, healthier, mature, complete in Christ. One decision today can completely change life.

Oh yes, I've made a lot of relational mistakes. I've hurt others and been hurt too. There have been times when I was ready to quit this journey and needed someone to tell me the ministry I was doing was valuable, helpful, significant. Other times I needed to simply believe the God I say I serve, and trust Him even more.

Growth is hard, good, and uncomfortable.

Today our values are still as important as when BENCHMARK began. They still provide a framework to aspire and embody:
- Spiritual formation and leadership development for all involved; participants, staff, volunteers, and founder.
- Commitment to be a debt-free ministry.
- Seeking strategic involvement, trusting God with the results.
- Speaking the truth, sometimes even in love.
- Acting in others' best interest.
- Making the most of every opportunity.

BENCHMARK has always been about people, not an organizational structure or location. The themes of pilgrim and aliens in the Bible remind me I'll not be on this planet long.

Although there were times when I questioned the decision to start a nonprofit and there were days when I didn't think BENCHMARK would make it to the end of the year, God has been faithful. So many people have been kind and faithful. I see God working it out in me over time and He is good. He's working His best out in others too.

AT THIS POINT

What brings a smile is that by the grace of God, the generosity of donors and volunteers, and a bit of stubbornness, this experiment called BENCHMARK Adventure Ministries continues.

Our mission is to stimulate significant life change toward wholeness in Christ. That . . . that makes getting up every day worth it.

Celebrate with us today.

AT THIS POINT

 May 27, 2019
Fifteen Minutes Matter

> *The key is not to prioritize what's on your schedule but to schedule your priorities.* – Stephen R. Covey[1]

Time is money . . . so some say.
No. It is not.
If I have all the money in the world, I can't purchase any more time. For those whose time is calculated in billable hours, there is a monetary connection to your use of time, but time is still not money. The commodities are very different.

In college, I wasted time. I had classes, multiple jobs, played intramural sports, had plenty to do yet still didn't use time well.

My daddy would write things down so he wouldn't forget them. I learned a great deal from Jonathan Thigpen, the main professor for my college major, and then made improvements. I began to calendar everything. Since I didn't have much money, I'd create my own four-and-a-half-month calendar each college semester on a single piece of poster board to plot out every assignment from every class I had and every due date. I didn't have a computer. I could see each week and month in one view, in an old school way. If I dropped an assignment it was because I wasn't looking at my calendar, not because I forgot.

Post college, I was trying to wrestle my time usage into submission. I continued to waste discretionary time, struggled with procrastination, and was easily distracted by . . . squirrel! Yes, all kinds of things. As a staff member of a small Christian Camp in

AT THIS POINT

eastern Kentucky, I needed to use time better, develop deeper spiritual disciplines, and watch less TV.

In about 1985, I attended my first conference of the organization which is now called Christian Camps and Conference Association. I signed up for an all-day early bird session called "The Organized Administrator." Wow! It was just what I needed. Not simply time management but personal, values-driven management. Then I began to use a system called Day-Timer®, which helped to put calendar, contacts, tasks, mileage, and expenses in one compact location. I started tracking every penny that God allowed to pass through my fingers. Every penny.

On my family Christmas list in 1991, I asked for The 7 Habits of Highly Effective People by Stephen R. Covey. My brother Joby and sister-in-law Carol bought it for me. Though my faith tradition is different from Stephen Covey's, his values-based, task/relationship model still affects my life and teaching, nearly thirty years later. Scheduling my priorities is critical.

So what about this fifteen-minutes idea?

In the application section of Covey's Habit 3, "Put First Things First," he suggests logging time usage for three days in fifteen-minute intervals. In an advanced level college class I taught for ministry students, I required them to log their time usage in fifteen-minute intervals for a whole week. It's a valuable assessment to visually see how a person uses time and then to move toward better aligning that usage with their stated priorities.

I've tried to be increasingly more mindful of how to use fifteen minutes well with a desire to use the next fifteen minutes wisely. I want to align my time usage with my priorities. Over time, fifteen minutes has shaped my thinking in many ways.

AT THIS POINT

The reason these fifteen minutes are important is because you only have those minutes once. There are really wonderful opportunities that only take fifteen minutes.

Sometimes people say, "I only have fifteen minutes."

Well, okay, use those fifteen minutes. What can I wisely do for fifteen minutes? Based on values and priorities, how can I choose to spend the next fifteen minutes?

My wife and I have four kids, now all grown up. We're past the most intense, hands-on part of parenting. Comparatively speaking, it's a pretty easy time for us.

But I still remember those times when it feels like the wheels are coming off, 'cause they were. Sick child, lack of sleep, trying to keep children from hurting themselves or others, the daily guidance that seems to never end, emotional reserve empty, trying to connect values to actions, attempting to figure out why this child is screaming.

Parenting leaves a mark.

Sometimes as a parent, I need to just not lose my mind for the next fifteen minutes. Or sometimes I need to pay attention to my child for the next fifteen minutes. Sometimes I need to not lose my temper just for the next fifteen minutes. And then after that, I need to not lose my temper for the next fifteen minutes. And when I do lose my temper, reset and start the clock again.

Fifteen minutes is just a snatch of time. But if we can leverage those fifteen minutes, sometimes it can help us move in a better direction.

Fifteen minutes matter. A person's whole life can change drastically with how they choose to use fifteen minutes for better, or for worse.

AT THIS POINT

I nap for fifteen minutes. When I go to bed at night and then lie awake for fifteen minutes, I get up and do something else. I'm apparently not tired enough to go to sleep.

For my spiritual and emotional well-being, I just sit, think, listen to the Bible, listen to a book or quality, life-giving podcast, or let an encouraging song play for the next fifteen minutes. Perhaps I journal or pray for fifteen minutes and set an alarm. Take a walk.

I set a timer to monitor my own social media or news app usage.

Fifteen minutes has been very helpful for me, just to check in and say, "Okay, what can I do well or what do I need to stop doing for the next fifteen minutes?" What's the best use of the next fifteen minutes?

I've used all manner of tools from paper to Palm Pilot to all sorts of apps, but the mindset is more important than the tool. Your priorities should manage your schedule.

I still get distracted. I do better than I did, but it's still an ongoing struggle. I need to use this next fifteen minutes wisely. Maybe it's time for me to track my time for the next three days.

So was your last fifteen minutes well spent?

How will you use the next fifteen minutes?

AT THIS POINT

 **June 5, 2020**
I Broke a Rib

On Saturday January 7, 2012, I was leading the team building/problem solving initiative called the horizontal web during BENCHMARK's leadership development retreat. As the instructor/leader of the initiative I decide to also become a participant without inserting my solution ideas.

I didn't jump as high as I needed to. My toe caught a cord that I was trying to avoid. When I came down, well, the ground was down there.

I got up, didn't think much of it, and I tried again.

Monday, two days later, I hiked 6.9 miles exploring Beaman Park with no discomfort. On Tuesday, I could hardly get out of bed. On Thursday I was off to my doctor who confirmed, "Yep, it's fractured." "If you take care of it, it will heal in eight weeks. If you don't, it will take longer." I guess my doc knew who he was talking to.

I have this conversation in my head. Actually I just ask myself a bunch of questions in quick succession, a cost/benefit analysis of sorts. Can I do it? What's keeping me from doing it? Am I able to do it or just don't want to do it? If I don't want to do it, should I do it anyway? Is someone telling me not to do something that I really can do? Is the price too high? Is the pain too great? Is it a price I'm willing to pay? What will it cost me long term?

I did what I was told. No physical activity for eight weeks. None. No YMCA weight training. No bike riding. Nothing. Just a reminder, in my world the first four months of the year are marathon training days. I needed to run. But I needed to not run. So I didn't.

AT THIS POINT

I hear I don't like to do what I'm told to do. But, I looked ahead and saw something more important than what I wanted to do now. And I wanted to be ready.

From the date of the fracture, I had exactly eight weeks before I'd be in the middle of a retreat with Chaplain Erik Alfsen and as many as twenty-four young, active male and female infantry Soldiers from the 187th Airborne Infantry Regiment of the 101st Airborne Division, Fort Campbell, Kentucky, the renowned "Rakkasans."

I wanted to invest in them well. And we were going on an adventure.

I did what my doctor instructed me to do, and I was ready for the retreat.

With instructional sessions and activities planned to slow them down, Saturday morning was horseback riding. After lunch we drove into the Great Smoky Mountains National Park to Lead Cove Trail on Little River Road at 1800' elevation. The summit of Rocky Top (5,441') is 5.9 miles one way, uphill. That's an 11.8 mile round trip.

At the intersection of the Bote Mountain and Anthony Creek Trails, I could see the frost way up on the ridge line. Hoarfrost happens when the moist rich air freezes on anything that sits still long enough. We were miles from the ridgeline but the temperature change up there was obvious.

It was going to be a stellar hike.

As we got to the ridgeline, it was beautiful, magical.

It's adventures like these that set the stage for potentially meaningful conversations and the development of lasting memories. If you don't do something you won't have something

AT THIS POINT

to talk about. It was a demanding hike finishing right where we began just as it was getting dark.

Just this morning (a few years after the fractured rib), I noticed again that place, that healed spot about middle way down on the right side of my rib cage. To this day, I feel a shallow something at the spot of that broken rib. It's not pain. It's not even discomfort. It's just there. I recognize it.

Physically, with time, care and sometimes intentionally not doing anything, we heal. The body is amazing. But there is still the memory of it. It reminds me of the past.

Still I wonder what that place would feel like today if I didn't take seriously what I was told to do or in this case, not do, to heal.

Seems over the years, I've collected a lot of those kinds of experiences. You know, those emotional and social fractures that remind me of the past. Some things just take some time to heal.

AT THIS POINT

 June 6, 2020
Worshiping Porcelain

I've been on a backcountry trip or two. I've heard a comment or two. It almost sounds like worship.

On more than one occasion I've heard people say, "I'm not an outdoorsy person."

Well, you don't have to be. I can live with that.

I've heard people talk about the bugs, and dirt, and sweat, and heat, and cold, and snakes, and spiders, and rain, and lightning. Some of those can kill you. Most don't.

Seems they miss the beauty, and detail, and quiet, and color, and creativity of creation.

More than one person has talked about their aversion to using the bathroom in the woods. There are books written on how to do it. Urination isn't so bad for most. Defecation seems to be a different deal.

Have you used a public bathroom at a sporting event or a gas station? How about a porta potty staged at some random public place?

If it weren't for social sensitivities and the management of waste on a large scale, I'd take the woods every time.

Taking care of that business one hundred and fifty feet from a road, trail, campsite, river or lake, well, it's cleaner and smells more pleasant than most public bathrooms or porta potties.

But it's the way people talk about a toilet and having it so readily available that gets my attention.

It almost sounds like worship.

I wonder if creature comforts keep you from following Christ into the uncomfortable?

AT THIS POINT

April 9, 2020
Fast & reFocus

These days are pretty unusual. Our schedules and daily demands are changing. For some, they have increased. For others, it's slowed way down. Either way, today is a good day to make a choice about how to make the most of the opportunity of a "day."

I want to ask you to do something that also may be unusual: Fast & reFocus. The Bible most often describes fasting as doing without food.

> More than any other single Discipline, fasting reveals the things that control us. This is a wonderful benefit to the true disciple who longs to be transformed into the image of Jesus Christ. We cover up what is inside us with food and other good things, but in fasting these things surface.
>
> Fasting helps us keep our balance in life. How easily we begin to allow nonessential to take precedence in our lives. How quickly we crave things we do not need until we are enslaved by them. – Richard Foster, Celebration of Discipline[1]

FAST

For this fast, I encourage you to reduce a different kind of consumption. We will use the New Testament guidance of "take off" and "put on." For a day, choose no social media or news

AT THIS POINT

broadcasts. None. "Take off" this influence for a day. Do without it.

Key question: What would be an appropriate challenge for you with your current circumstances?

Then, pick a day. Maybe you choose Good Friday, or maybe another day works better for you in the next seven days. You get to choose how you define "day."

Yes, there are some wonderful aspects of social media and news. I am not suggesting we choose to be uninformed. I am suggesting we can all get drawn into the less admirable and spend entirely too much time there.

reFOCUS

Instead reFOCUS on what is life giving. Put on good music or a good movie. Read a book that will help you to align your heart with God's heart and His purposes for the world. Choose media for the day where the content will most likely be admirable. Choose one of these stories of Christ and schedule time to read it: Matthew 26–27, Mark 14:12–15:47, Luke 22–24, John 18–19. You could take in a Good Friday church broadcast or live stream. Make the best choice you can in the middle of whatever else is a normal day for you.

Define the "day." Commit to it.

If you fail, acknowledge it. Or maybe, when you fail.

Ask yourself, "Why did I 'fail'?" Consider what's at the root of the "failure." Look it in the eye.

Forgive yourself. Repent, if for some reason that's needed. Recommit. Start again.

AT THIS POINT

Isn't that the heart of the Gospel? Acknowledge. Seek forgiveness. Start again.

After you've completed your day, if you'd like, please tell us how it went.

AT THIS POINT

 May 9, 2020
Eleven Minutes

Will you plan to spend eleven minutes tomorrow on this Good Friday reflection?

1. Use three minutes to consider the significance of someone who is willing to lay down his or her life for you. Think about a parent, a first responder, a Soldier, even a stranger. What do you think would motivate such a person?

2. Use one minute to write your thoughts.

3. Use three minutes to consider that Jesus came to earth knowing He would lay down His life as the full payment for your sin. He came to live and die so that we would not bear the responsibility or guilt of sin, if we repent. He knew the great cost yet He came anyway.

4. Use one minute to write your confession of sin.

5. With an eye toward Easter Sunday, and because of Christ's example, use 1 minute to think about a simple act of service you can do, a very small act of laying your life down.

6. Take two minutes to serve someone else in Jesus Christ's name and because of His example.

This is how my eleven minutes went.
*Potentially Too Much Information

AT THIS POINT

My scheduled eleven minutes was interrupted twice. The first by a friend who I talk to regularly but has some significant family stuff going on. He calls when he can talk so I took the call. I rescheduled time and sat down to focus for eleven minutes. Barbara, my wife called. She is making a two-hour trip today to visit a college with my daughter. They hadn't been gone that long so I "ignored" the call and told her I couldn't talk right now. She texted and then called back.

I knew something was up. The bumper was flapping in the wind and she was concerned it was trying to come off the van from a previous fender bender. She was on the interstate shoulder needing advice. My eleven minutes were getting interrupted by someone I needed to serve. I found that I was grumpy for the interruption, not grumpy to help my wife. There was a tension between trying to focus on my scheduled time and other demands. Does anyone care that I'm trying to have time with Jesus, to reflect, to consider His life of service through death and resurrection?

I'm confident that Jesus laid down His life and wasn't grumpy about it because He had such great love for me. I, on the other hand, am still trying to work it out.

AT THIS POINT

 May 24, 2020
4x4x48: Toward Birthday Endurance

> . . . *and you know what power a dare has on a weak mind.* – Michael Card[1]

> *So whether you eat or drink or whatever you do, do it all for the glory of God.*
> (1 Corinthians 10:31)

My birthday is May 20th. Some come and some go. Some are fun and enjoyable. Some are more dutiful, more normal. Mostly it's good to see another day and I'm glad I was born.

When I turned twelve-years old, my friend Eric Mallard gave me a twenty-eight-inch Little League approved Carl Yastrzemski wooden baseball bat for my birthday. It was a good birthday. Earlier that same year I was hit by a truck while riding my bicycle. Maybe somewhere in the back crevasses of my mind it gave me some hope that I would one day play baseball again. I am proud enough of that bat that it still hangs in my office.

About a week after I graduated from Wheaton College Graduate School I turned 26 years old. My parents and my fiancée had driven to Chicago for the graduation ceremony. It was mid-May, and in a couple short weeks I would be marrying Barbara in Nashville. I was in my final days as a single man so I went to hike some miles on Cumberland Island, Georgia, so my heart and mind could catch up to my body.

My twenty-eighth birthday I spent being a student on a sixteen-day wilderness trip in northern Wisconsin and the Upper Peninsula of Michigan. Then starting in 1992, I spent the next seven

AT THIS POINT

birthdays in the woods leading sixteen-day wilderness trips with Wheaton College/Honey Rock High Road. It's a great way to celebrate.

Again, some come and go. Regular work. Kids. Family. It's OK. They don't have to all be "special."

My thirtieth and fortieth came and went, at least I remember them as such. My fiftieth was hard. My wife and family threw me a birthday party. It's important to note that for fifty years I have been a teetotaler, choosing not to drink alcohol. There are all kinds of reasons why I have made that choice. It's not a judgment of you, it's a choice by me. I don't drink alcohol.

That evening, I remember telling my wife while standing in our kitchen with guests outside, "I think I'm now old enough." She said, "Old enough for what?" "I think I am old enough to begin drinking . . . heavily."

She didn't think that was a good idea.

It wasn't a good idea, but it wasn't a good day either. Things in my head and heart were piling up. In time, I spent some planned time with friends and a therapist to work through some things I thought were settled. Or at least they were, and then they came back, like one of those yippy, ankle-biting dogs that keep nipping at your heels.

May 20, 2020

We would celebrate our youngest daughter Hannah's graduation from high school. In the season of the Coronavirus/COVID-19, it was to be a drive-by graduation. She and I agreed what food we'd enjoy together for her graduation and my birthday. Because the day had gotten away from us, we

AT THIS POINT

ate Panda Express, a favorite of mine. Her choice of Blue Coast Burrito would wait till lunch the next day since it had already closed for the day.

We stepped toward her graduation believing that the plans were the best that the school and school board could make with the moving target of guidelines, fear, and uncertainty. We were going to make the best of it. For a drive-by graduation, it was very personal, and one of the best graduations of any of our kids.

Since BENCHMARK and I had more empty space on the calendar than we wanted, I was looking for a way to use the time well. I didn't want what I wanted to do to adversely impact my daughter's graduation celebration. How to spend my birthday in 2020 was influenced by someone I met earlier in the year.

In February 2020, BENCHMARK served fifty-three leadership team members of the 1-187 Infantry Battalion, 101st Airborne from Fort Campbell, Kentucky. I met John who was responsible for the unit's morning physical training (PT) event. Captain John Bergman is a kind, exceptionally bright, and ridiculously fit Soldier.

During the retreat, I learned John was that John Bergman, a two-time winner of the Best Ranger Competition[2] held yearly at Fort Benning, Georgia. I've been a spectator a couple of times at the Best Ranger Competition. Winning once is an incredible feat of physical endurance, emotional toughness, intellectual capacity, and Ranger skill. Winning twice is unbelievable.

The next morning I joined the unit on the run CPT Bergman laid out; up to the road, around the sloppy, muddy state park loop trail and back to the camp where the Soldiers had additional physical training in a field.

Standing by a campfire that evening chatting with Soldiers, drinking IBC Root beer and roasting marshmallows by a large

AT THIS POINT

enough fire, John stopped by. We chatted a bit. I told him that "if I was a fanboy, and I am not, I'd follow him around." We also talked about James Rutland, an instinct shooting trainer, who was a part of the retreat using BB guns to improve shooter accuracy and hand/eye coordination. John had benefited from James Rutland before his first Best Ranger Competition. John wanted me to better introduce Mr. Rutland, his skill, his capabilities, and the value he could be to the Soldiers.

I said to John, "You and Mr. Rutland are a lot alike. Neither of you want to be called out for your abilities."

A little over a month after the February retreat, John Bergman invited me, out of the blue, to the 1-187 Infantry Battalion, Bulldog Company's Endurathon.

> The event provides anyone the opportunity to take an introductory step into the realm of mentally challenging endurance sports. It is based off of motivational speaker, David Goggins' 4x4x48 concept.
>
> The 3x3x12 Bulldog Endurathon is simple. Run, ruck, or walk 3 miles, every 3 hours, for 12 hours, for a total of 5 sets. The final set starts at the 12-hour mark. After fifteen miles are complete, you've completed the challenge. Anyone can participate, but only Bulldog Soldiers can compete for prizes/awards.
>
> Good luck on Monday, and can't wait to see you there!

AT THIS POINT

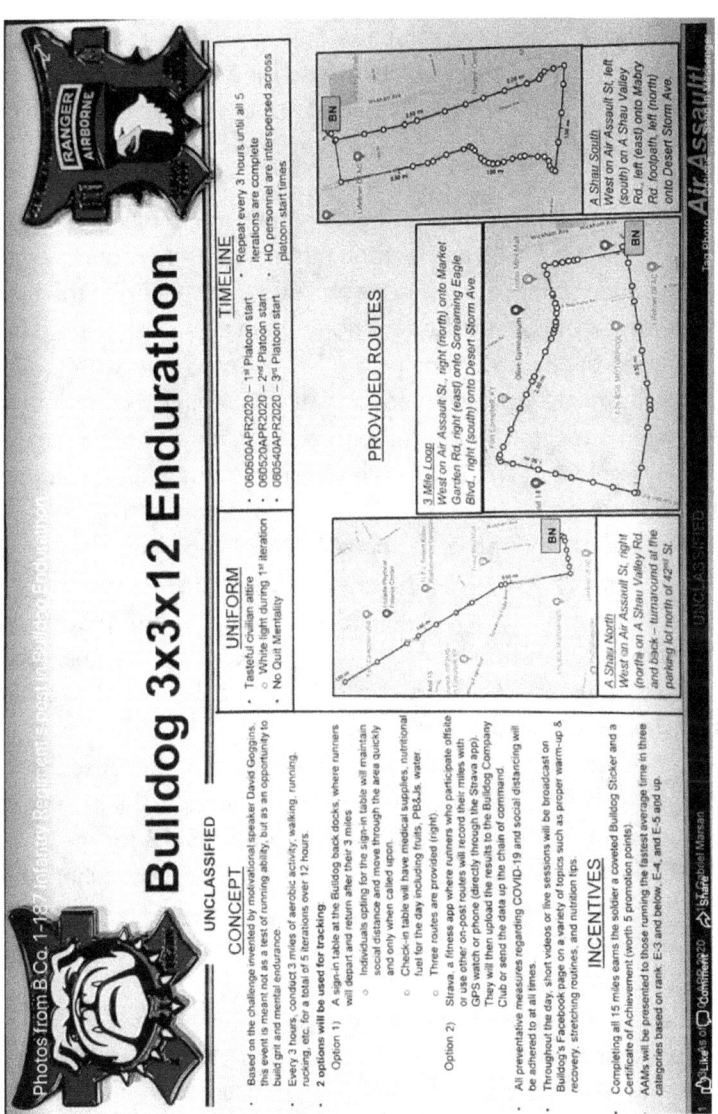

AT THIS POINT

I reached out: "John, I absolutely would drive to Fort Campbell to be a part of this on Monday. Thank you for the invitation. With the current COVID-19 cautions, would I be allowed to get on post at 4:30am? Must I rely on more remote Strava participation? What do you think?"

After a bit of back and forth with him online, it made sense for me to stay in Nashville and use the mobile app since John was not on post and most everyone in his unit was teleworking at the time.

Monday, April 6th, the Endurathon began at 6 a.m. I started and completed the 3x3x12, running 3 miles every 3 hours with the last 3 miles at the 12-hour mark for a total of 15 miles. I completed it well, even after I ran 19 miles for my regular marathon training just two days before. It was a good challenge but not the hardest thing I had ever done.

The seed thought of a 4x4x48 David Goggins Challenge, running 4 miles every 4 hours for 48 hours, had sprouted.

A few weeks later I received by mail a Bulldog Company challenge coin and Bulldog Company sticker. The coin has been added to my modest military challenge coin collection. The sticker is on the BENCHMARK truck.

I reached out to John and told him that because of his "previous invitation to the Bulldog Endurathon, I'm thinking about whatever might be the second iteration of 3x3x12 for me. I had the thought of a 4x4x48 but I may have been delirious when I had that thought."

John said, "I'm impressed with you, hoping to still get after it when I grow up."

Yep, the fanboy in me smiled. But there is also something deeper going on. Why would arguably one of the fittest and most resilient human beings I've ever met (and I've met a few) pay any

AT THIS POINT

attention to a middle-aged man like me? It says more about the quality of human being, Army infantry officer, and follower of Jesus Christ that John Bergman is. Maybe I want to be like John when I grow up.

That seed thought of a 4x4x48 grew from interactions with re a and Sean O'Brien. Sean, aka "The Metronome," who runs with the neighborhood running group, can hold a per mile pace more consistently than anyone else I've run with. On April 26th, Sean and a buddy of his ran 4.166 miles every hour for 12 hours for a total of 50 miles. Donna, another accomplice in our running groups, ran 35 miles with Sean in about 9 hours. The day before, Saturday, April 25th, was the COVID-19-canceled Rock and Roll Nashville Marathon. I ran it anyway, unofficially, of course. It would have just been ridiculous for me to try to run with Sean on his 50-miler. My wife Barbara and I happened to catch up with them on our bikes for the last mile or so.

Since my youngest daughter's graduation plans were almost worked out, I couldn't commit to a run of much length on my birthday. I didn't want my plans to bump into hers. High school graduation is still a big deal. And she is the last of our children to do so.

On my birthday, but more importantly, Hannah's graduation day, a family friend, Tracy, and her two kids stopped by. They were bringing a graduation card and gift to Hannah and thoughtfully brought a quirky birthday card to me which said:

"Getting older is kinda like frying bacon in the nude. You know it's gonna hurt, but you're not exactly sure where. Happy birthday!"

Tracy wrote in the card: "James, the truth hurts – literally. Especially when you are a legacy runner and still do your 26.2 even

AT THIS POINT

though the marathon is canceled!!! We hope your 58th is free of pain and pandemics – enjoyable. We know it will be special spending this day celebrating Hannah's graduation! Enjoy it!"

Since Tracy is a runner, I told her I had been thinking about a 4x4x48 but didn't know when I'd do it.

When she and her kids left, out the door I went to run 5.8 miles on my 58th birthday, which seems reasonable to me. Why would I try to run 58 miles on my birthday? Why not? While on that run, I started to think seriously about the 4x4x48. We knew the graduation plans but I was fairly sure I couldn't start that night, since I was currently running 5.8. I had not planned this very well.

On the running shoe of my right foot I have a ROAD iD®, "safety identification tags and bracelets for runner id, cyclist id, medical id, bicycling id, and emergency medical id." In the event of an emergency, there is some helpful information for a first responder or by-stander who lends assistance. It has my name, the year of my birth, city, state, zip. It also lists the names and phone numbers of three very important people who may need to know that my world just changed; Barbara WIFE, Kinley BRO, Christopher SON. All that's emergency information.

The last line is my personal daily encouragement information simply stated: "Do What You Can Do."

At the end of my 5.8-mile run, my friend and BENCHMARK Board member and former Board chair called. We talked about whatever he called about and then I told him what I was thinking. At that point, I had not told my wife. Mike Gingras said, "Let me know what you decide."

I checked a weather app which forecasted cooler than normal May days with some chance of rain, even storms, but not until

AT THIS POINT

Saturday noon. It looked very promising. I decided to tell my wife what I was thinking.

The next morning, without prompting, my wife came to me with an idea. "What you could do is run 4.143 miles every 4 hours 30 minutes and you'd get to 58." Yep, she knows me well.

I had been thinking about running 58 miles already for my 58th birthday. I hadn't told her. I really wanted to finish the 4x4x48 as Goggins laid it out, then if I could do that, I'd decide if I wanted to push to 58 miles.

When my wife starts feeding what some call "crazy," I know I'm on the right path. Oh, by the way, I don't call it "crazy."

Around here I call it normal.

AT THIS POINT

 May 24, 2020
4x4x48: Toward Physical Resilience

In case you're wondering, our daughter's graduation was really good. From a parent's perspective, it may have been the most simple, enjoyable, and personal public-school high school graduation I had ever attended. Members of the faculty, staff and even the principal called her by name and passed along happy greetings. Hume-Fogg Academic High School did a wonderful job.

By 11 p.m. on the night of my birthday I was sending this announcement out to friends.

> I'm stepping toward a physical and mental endurance challenge. It's a 4x4x48 made popular by David Goggins, a retired Navy Seal. The 4x4x48 is four miles every four hours in forty-eight hours. I plan to run at 4 p.m./a.m., 8 p.m./a.m., 12 midnight/noon. First run: 4 p.m. Thursday. Last run: Saturday noon. I'll start and end very near my house, rain or shine. If you're faster than me, slow down. If you are slower than me, I have a bike you can borrow. I want to celebrate the life of living warriors, ministers and servants with an eye on Memorial Day when we remember those who gave all. Come run with me.

The next morning, I sent the message to some other "normal" people in the 38th Ave North running group led by Bill. This group has kindly challenged my typical pace and pushed me to get

AT THIS POINT

faster...and that's just because I'm trying to keep up with them. The message to this group began with, "Sean and Donna have shown the way. I'm stepping toward a physical and mental endurance... "

See, I have some friends who, by their example, challenge what I think I can do mentally and physically. Sometimes I join them. Sometimes they join me.

Run #1 - Mike, a BENCHMARK Board member, and Donna, part of the 38th Ave North Running Crew, came for the first run at 4 p.m.

Run #2 - Kinley, my best friend, came for every 8 p.m. run and bonus run #2.

Run #3 - Tracy, the graduation gift and birthday card deliverer, looked at her family commitments and decided to run her first miles ever at night, at midnight, trusting me enough to join me.

Run #4 - Danielle and Sarah came for run #4, the first 4 a.m. run.

Run #5 - I ran alone, thinking about SSG Ryan Davis of the 1st Battalion, 75th Ranger Regiment, who had been catastrophically injured in Afghanistan nine months before. I posted a simple message on the "Run for Ryan" Facebook group, May 22 at 11:00 AM:

> Yesterday I began a series of runs. Today on my 4 a.m. run #4 and 8 a.m. run #5 I wore the U.S. Army Ranger Crest thinking about the tenacity, perseverance and personal courage of Ryan . . . and Asia. Though we have not met, I know a couple of Ranger Chaplains you know. I've been

AT THIS POINT

encouraged by the beauty and simplicity of Asia's handwritten Scripture (red ink on simple brown paper) and her commitment to Ryan's hard journey. I am challenged by Ryan's work ethic, heart, and strength.

"Finally, be strong in the Lord and in his mighty power." Ephesians 6:10

Ryan and his wife, Asia, responded kindly.

Run #6 - Danielle came back at noon. I wore my 160th Special Operations Aviation Regiment "Death Waits in the Dark" shirt given to me by retired U.S. Army Chaplain, Major Jay Tobin.

Run #7 - Mike and Donna ran again, the second 4 p.m. run, along with child #2, daughter #1, Elizabeth who was home from college before she headed to a camp staff role. Elizabeth rode her bike.

Run #8 - Kinley returned for 8 p.m.

Run #9 - Midnight, I ran alone.

Run #10 - Jonathan, child #3, son #2, was scheduled for work early on Saturday morning. He told me the night before that he was going to get up and go on my 4 a.m. run. He'd ride his bike. As we were getting ready I received a text at 3:53am from Jon Betts, "I don't want to startle you at 3:50 in the morning but I just thought you might want someone to run with so I am out front." What a delightful surprise.

Run #11 - My working nurse wife, Barbara, joined Sarah and I for run #11, 8am. This was Sarah's second run as an "accomplice," her good word choice.

AT THIS POINT

With my last 4x4x48 run in sight, I texted the 38th Ave N/Bill's Running Group that I had decided to attempt ten more miles; five miles each at 4 p.m. and 8 p.m. These days had been so good with 9 of the 11 runs having an "accomplice." I thanked Danielle, Donna and Sarah and others outside Bill's crew, for the encouragement and unexpected running support that made the miles better.

Run #12 - Barbara rode her bike again at noon. The 83° day was warmer than the previous days.

Barbara asked the most puzzling question while I was struggling to run just 4 more miles. "What are you going to do next?"

My answer, "Finish this run."

She probably thought I was thinking about what was next. But all I could do, or wanted to do, was to finish.

I finished my first official 4x4x48. More on that later in the post run reflections.

During the days of the 4x4x48, May 21-23, Hannah, child #4, daughter #2, and I continued our daily 1-mile walks numbers 48-50. It was a daddy/daughter activity we had started weeks before.

Five-Mile Bonus Run #1 / Run #13 - Barbara traded her bike in for her running shoes at 4 p.m. Donna came back with a smile for her third 4 p.m. run. It was 86°. Cool temps for some. Warm for me. I was slowing down.

Five-Mile Bonus Run #2 / Run #14 - The final, final at 8 p.m. was celebrated with the largest crew of people; Barbara, Mike, Kinley and Elizabeth. It had cooled to 81°. I was slower still.

But...done.

Fifty-eight point seventy-nine (58.79) miles in fifty-three hours, plus the May 20th run, and the walks with my daughter, I covered

AT THIS POINT

69.31 miles in eighty hours. Though I backpacked 70.5 miles of the Appalachian Trail through the Great Smoky Mountains National Park in about fifty-eight hours, this was the most miles I had run or walked in the shortest amount of time. Done is good.

Not being "done," before you finish, is better.

I thought I'd be running mostly alone and continue a writing project. I stepped toward those hours with a clear focus to pray for and celebrate the life of living warriors, ministers and servants. But whatever plan I had…changed, wonderfully changed, with the unexpected support of so many.

People came to encourage and join my journey. Those in front of me became the priority.

AT THIS POINT

Temp	Date		Run #	Time	Time	Mileage	Accomplices	/mile
	James' 4x4x48							
	May 20th	my 58th birthday						
	May 20th			11:43am		5.8	~	8:25
	4x4x48 Begins							
	TR, May 21		1	4pm	1600	4.25	Donna, Mike	8:55
			2	8pm	2000	4.11	Kinley	9:39
	FRI, May 22		3	Midnight	0000	4.01	Tracy	8:57
			4	4am	0400	4.00	Danielle, Sarah	8:47
			5	8am	0800	4.08	~	8:42
			6	Noon	1200	4.11	Danielle	8:41
			7	4pm	1600	4.08	Donna, Mike, Elizabeth	8:45
			8	8pm	2000	4.02	Kinley	8:54
	SAT, May 23		9	Midnight	0000	4.00	~	9:26
			10	4am	0400	4.00	Jon, Jonathan	9:02
			11	8am	0800	4.03	Sarah, Barbara	8:47
83°			12	Noon	1200	4.01	Barbara	9:37
	4x4x48 Ends					48.70		9:01
86°	Bonus Run		1	4pm	0400	5.08	Barbara, Donna	10:46
81°	Bonus Run		2	8pm	0800	5.01	Barbara, Mike, Kinley, Elizabeth	11:00
						10.09		
	Daddy Daughter 1 mile Walks							
	May 21		48	5:15pm		1.49	Hannah	
	May 22		49	9:49pm		1.6	Hannah, Barbara	
	May 23		50	6:14pm		1.69	Hannah, Elizabeth	
						4.78		
First Goal:		48 miles in 48 hours				48.7	in 45 hours	
Second Goal:		58 miles in 58 hours				58.79	in 53 hours	
	Total Movement Miles:					63.57		
	4 day miles		May 20th			5.8		
						69.37		

Over those next fifty-three hours, the journey was far better than I thought it would be. Of the fourteen total runs I did, only two I ran alone. Ten different people took the time to go with me (some ran, some biked) for one or more sections, including two of my kids who were home and my wife Barbara Allen Evans (8 a.m., noon, 4 p.m., 8 p.m.). Other accomplices were Mike Gingras (4 p.m., 4 p.m., 8 p.m. runs), Donna Smailis (4 p.m., 4 p.m., 4 p.m.),

AT THIS POINT

Kinley Winchester (8 p.m., 8 p.m., 8 p.m.), Tracy Eckert (midnight), Danielle Hunt (4 a.m., Noon), Sarah Welch (4 a.m., 8 a.m.), Elizabeth Evans (4 p.m., 8 p.m.), Jon Betts (4 a.m.), Jonathan Evans (4 a.m.).

And though I did think of Jay Tobin, Dana Krull, SSG Ryan Davis, SGT Tom Block and B Co. 3/75th, Ken Kalisch and Kirk Adkisson, to name a few, I didn't take time to reach out to them all. Preparing for the next 4 miles became my priority. By Saturday my life was run, cool down, talk to friends who ran, eat, shower, sleep, alarm rings at 20 minutes till, get ready to run, rinse, repeat. I slept no more than 2 hours 15 minutes at a time.

Another example of when my plan was superseded by…a better plan.

What did I learn or confirm so far? [Look in the next chapter.]

I'm a grateful man.

I finished the 4x4x48 averaging 9:01/mile, a one second per mile average slower than my 9:00 minute per mile goal. The miles, lack of sleep, and heat took its toll and I did the next ten miles at a slower pace. From May 20th through 23rd, I ran 5.8 miles on my birthday, 48.7 miles for the 4x4x48, plus 5.08, plus 5.01 miles and three Daddy Daughter one-mile walks, #48, #49 and #50, totaling 4.78 miles to maintain our streak. My total movement for four days was 69.37 miles.

Not bad for an old man, huh?

AT THIS POINT

 May 9, 2020
4x4x48: Toward Life Change

What did I learn or confirm because of the 4x4x48? Here's an expanded look.

1. Drink your water.
From my P90X and P90X3 days, I hear Tony Horton saying "Drink your waaater." It's good advice that dog piles onto my regular habit. I learned a lot of years ago that every cell in my body needs water to function properly and that most people live in a constant state of dehydration. I drink water. It is possible to drink too much, but most don't drink enough.

I don't drink coffee or high energy drinks with added caffeine. I drink some decaffeinated tea, of course sweet tea, because I'm a Southern boy, and occasionally hot tea. I drink a few sugary soft drinks with Sonic® strawberry limeade, a favorite. When training, and pushing long running or hiking miles, I drink water with electrolytes. I drink mostly water because it's good for my body, mind…and every cell in my body.

There have been many times when a trip participant comes to me with a headache and wants a pill to ease the discomfort. I'd ask them if they would try something for me, "Drink a quart of water in the next hour and then let me know if your headache persists." Most don't come back. When I ask, their headache is most often gone. If it's not, then something else may be going on. Water is magical and vital because it's critical for every body to function well.

AT THIS POINT

2. I am still active by the abundant grace of God and regular conditioning.

There was a spiritual discipline of prayer that I did for some time. It was split into "My Part" and "God's Part." It's stuck with me for years. God has a part. I have a part. I can't do God's part. Though there is much God the Father can do and often does do, there are things He chooses not to do. God doesn't make me put on my hiking boots and backpack, and reach for my hiking stick, or get on my mountain bike. God doesn't tie the laces of my running shoes. He doesn't make me do the stretching this aging body benefits from. That's my choice, and choices have consequences. Some consequences are known as benefits. My life circumstances allow for wide freedom.

But I live out grace. Health I do not deserve. A home I do not deserve. Opportunities I have worked toward but do not deserve. I am not entitled to them. But if it weren't for the abundant grace of God, a perplexing undeserved gift that I do not control, my life would change in a moment. Air wouldn't be breathable. Gravity would fail. Water wouldn't work. I could want it all I want; it just wouldn't matter.

3. My adventurous life helped to prepare me for this challenge.

Running for thirty years, wilderness trips being mentally stretched, and short nights of sleep for all kinds of great and potentially ridiculous reasons has helped. Sticking to a schedule of weekly runs for months to train for twenty-one marathons over twenty-one years . . . helps. Pushing myself to see what I could do and figuring out I can go a little bit more, maybe slower, and at times, maintain a good attitude. That helps. Parenting for twenty-five years helps. Our history matters. Our choices matter.

AT THIS POINT

4. Two hotdogs with ketchup, mustard and relish at 9:30 p.m. between runs #8 and #9 is a really bad idea.
   It made sense at the time. I was hungry. I like the periodic hot dog. It's "comfort food." I wasn't putting anything into my body that I hadn't eaten before. But . . . it was a bad idea, a really bad idea, that I was reminded of on run #9 and run #10 at 4 a.m.

5. I have some wonderful friends who continue to support what some think is crazy.
   If I had a nickel for every time I've been called "crazy," I'd be . . . well, I'll let you finish the sentence. Some have joined willingly. Others find themselves where they aren't sure they want to be. I've been called crazy by all kinds of people to my face. But I'm pretty sure I'm not. Toleration of who I am as a person is one response. Joining me is a better one.

6. Training is about recovery.
   I may struggle to finish a marathon with much speed, and have also thrown up whatever I put in my stomach right after a race. An afternoon nap, food, water with electrolytes, a good night's sleep, and I'm, most often, doing pretty well by Sunday morning. The Hal Higdon Marathon Training Program running 4 days a week for 18 weeks helps to train the body and mind. Regimented training helps. Learning from other people about training prepares the body toward recovery.

7. Running in hot temperatures takes it out of me.
   The last weekend of April is the date for the Country Music Marathon whose name recently changed to the Rock and Roll

AT THIS POINT

Nashville. When it's warm, my slower than elite pace puts me on the marathon course for longer than 4 hours approaching 11 a.m. At mile 23 of a marathon, 3.2 more miles can feel like a very, very long way. On the days when it's around 80 degrees, those miles feel even longer.

The daytime Saturday heat for the 4x4x48 got in my head. My legs were heavy. I was ready to stop. I had decided at 8 a.m. that I would push to 58 miles. At noon it was 83°. I was seriously questioning the idea to push to 58 miles. I was dreaming up my excuses to tell those I had already told I'd be doing more miles. I walked a little. The sun was beating on me. When I finished the 48 miles at almost the same time of day I finish a marathon, I was not looking forward to the next ten miles. The 5 miles at 4 p.m. was 86°. The 8 p.m. run was 81°. Heat takes it out of me.

But I resolved to finish. Yogi Berra said "Baseball is 90% mental and the other half is physical." Seems I'm still working on the mental part of life and running.

8. Sometimes you still need more water.

I have been in a few places where I was really, really thirsty. In the backcountry, a water source sometimes doesn't work out where I want it to be or where the map shows it's supposed to be. Doing without has made me thankful I have accessible water. I want to use it wisely. Though I can waste some too, it's a rare thing for me to waste much. Not only is water down the drain, money is down the drain and it's wasting a precious resource.

You can do without water…for a time. And too much water is too much.

Remember, water is magical…and vital.

AT THIS POINT

9. I do a lot by myself, and will continue to do so. But it is difficult to overstate the benefit of the right people on the journey at the right time.

I've run, biked, and hiked a lot of miles alone, at all hours of the day and night. Much of the work I do on a daily basis I do alone. It is the rare occasion when I hesitate to get something done because no one else is around. I don't have to have someone around in order to get tasks completed. I don't have to have someone around to motivate me, most of the time. I don't have to have an audience in order to get things done. There are a lot of things that would never get done if I waited on others to join me.

But, it is difficult to overstate the benefit of the right people on the journey at the right time. People who decide to run your pace when they can run faster, when your pace gets even slower. People who alter their plans to join the "crazy," just to help you see what you can do. The word of encouragement they bring from their lips and by their presence is huge.

10. The example of others, who are living life well in the middle of or after really hard life events, encourages and challenges me to keep moving.

I did think of several people and prayed for a few both before and during this endurance event.

I think often of Jay Tobin, retired Chaplain (Major) with his wife Robin raising 4 adopted kids; Dana Krull, honorably discharged former infantry officer and Ranger Chaplain currently living in Ohio; SSG Ryan Davis who was severely injured in an August 2019 raid in Afghanistan; SGT Tom Block, who was injured October 5, 2013 in southern Afghanistan; and Soldiers I have met and

AT THIS POINT

mourned with from B Co, 3rd Battalion/75th Ranger Regiment; Ken Kalisch, a long-time friend; Kirk Adkisson, pastoring in North Nashville.

That list expands rapidly with just a pause.

It's the example of others, who have trod a hard path and appear to be doing it well, oftentimes with joy and hope for the future, that challenges me to keep moving. If they can work through life after it has hit the fan, perhaps I can too.

11. I wish I would have started taking pictures of the running groups earlier.

I take some selfies but my selfies normally include other people. Not sure I even like the term "selfie" but that is a different quirk. In this case, I missed the opportunity to take a photo with some of the people who shifted their schedules to join mine.

I didn't take selfies of Donna and Mike on run #1, Kinley on run #2, Tracy at midnight, Danielle and Sarah at 4 a.m. and Danielle at noon. Those were all selfies worth taking . . . and I missed capturing the snapshot. Bummer.

12. A sense of humor helps. Mine slipped away from time to time.

With the miles and lack of sleep, the conflict of the mind, spirit and emotions emerges. Am I keeping my pace, or is it just OK that I'm doing what I'm doing at the pace I'm doing it? The questions and circumstances of life that creep in and distract. 'Nough said.

In my very first invitation to join my very first 4x4x48, I was running because "I want to celebrate the life of living warriors, ministers, and servants with an eye on Memorial Day when we remember those who gave all."

AT THIS POINT

With a celebration of life and endurance done, my attention shifted to those who gave the last full measure of devotion.

I've only met one young Soldier who died in active military service. His name is Army PFC Cody J. Patterson. He sat beside me during a small group discussion on a July 2013 retreat. Three months later, he was gone. I don't know his loss nearly as deeply as his family, friends, and those he served with. But I remember.

Cody died on October 6, 2013, along with 1st Lt. Jennifer M. Moreno, Sgt. Patrick C. Hawkins, and Sgt. Joseph M. Peters. It's the same night Sgt. Tom Block and nearly two dozen were injured on October 5, 2013.

I know many others who mourn deeply on Memorial Day and on birthdays, anniversaries, and holidays because they know deeply the sadness and loss to never be able to talk to their loved one or friend again in this life. They remember.

And since they remember, I need to be reminded.

AT THIS POINT

 July 8, 2020
Things I Don't Like

When I'm right and I can't convince anyone else I am.

When I'm right and I'm right.

When I'm wrong and don't know it and no one tells me…kindly.

When I'm wrong and don't know it and no one tells me…harshly.

When I'm wrong and don't know it and no one tells me…at all.

The feeling of a rug slowly moving on my bathroom floor underneath my foot.

AT THIS POINT

 July 20, 2020
Be Still or Act

It is a natural, normal, human tendency to want to control. I struggle with it. I keep trying to collect wisdom that moves me to rely on God and act in a way that honors Him.

Sometimes I am to be still.
Sometimes I am to act.

Sometimes I am to act and then be still.
Sometimes I am to be still and then act.

Sometimes I am to humbly act and then boldly be still.
Sometimes I am to be humbly still and then boldly act.

Sometimes I am to boldly act and then humbly be still.
Sometimes I am to be boldly still and then humbly act.

I'm still working on working it out.
May God grant me wisdom.

Still
Written by Reuben Morgan

[Verse 1]
Hide me now
Under Your wings
Cover me

AT THIS POINT

Within Your mighty hand

[Chorus]
When the oceans rise and thunders roar
I will soar with You above the storm
Father, You are King over the flood
I will be still, know You are God

[Verse 2]
Find rest my soul
In Christ alone
Know His power
In quietness and trust

[Chorus]
When the oceans rise and thunders roar
I will soar with You above the storm
Father, You are King over the flood
I will be still, know You are God
When the oceans rise and thunders roar
I will soar with You above the storm
Father, You are King over the flood
I will be still, know You are God

[Post-Chorus]
Know You are God, oh yeah
Know You are God, oh know You are God
Know You are God, know You are God

[Interlude]

AT THIS POINT

[Verse 2]
Find rest my soul
In Christ alone
Know His power
In quietness and trust

[Chorus]
When the oceans rise and thunders roar
I will soar with You above the storm (Oh, yes I will)
Father, You are King over the flood
And I will be still, know You are God
When the oceans rise and thunders roar
I will soar with You above the storm (Yes I will, yes I will)
Father, You are King over the flood
And I will be still, know You are God
When the oceans rise and thunders roar
I will soar with You above the storm
Father, You are King over the flood
I will be still, know You are God

[Outro]
Oh, yes You are, oh, yes You are
Oh God, oh God
I will be still, oh God[1]

AT THIS POINT

 November 19, 2021
Gratitude
2021 Fort Campbell Thanksgiving Dinner Address

I lead a nonprofit which is made possible by donors, servants, notecard writers, and adventurers. A few of us are here to serve you. We are here today not for what we want from you but because of what we want for you. The majority of our service is joyful as we partner with U.S. Army Chaplains to serve the Soldiers they serve.

A brief personal introduction may be helpful for context. My name is James. The most important thing you need to know about me is that I am a hard-headed, imperfect follower of Jesus Christ. The second most important thing is, I'm not here to push my faith tradition down your throat. I am very serious about the work of this ministry, my faith, how I lead my life, and the quality of our work. Very…serious. But I'm also just straight up silly, and sarcasm runs about hip deep in my world. So good luck trying to keep up. I'm serious, silly, and sarcastic because I want you to pay attention to an old guy who is still vertical.

Because I realize to whom I get to speak to this afternoon, and I know I'm the guy who stands between you and a good meal, I am keenly aware that I have twenty minutes, plus or minus thirty seconds. Oh, wait, now I only have nineteen minutes. So let's get to it.

Commander, Command Sergeant Major, all those with all those deployment stripes on your dress blues, Permanent Party, and Cadre, and Family Members, I'm honored to be here with you.

Students, I'm glad to see you could get out of the basement this afternoon. You're welcome.

AT THIS POINT

Today I get to talk to you about gratitude. "Get to" and gratitude are closely connected ideas. In order to get to gratitude I need to take a tangent.

Gratitude is contrasted against a stark reality. Are you ready?

None of us will get through this life unscathed, unhurt, without trouble or suffering. No one. We'll either do it to ourselves, someone will do it to us, or it will come on its own.

That, my friends, is the real news. It is faulty thinking and false hope to think otherwise.

A key to living a life of gratitude is to make the most of every opportunity, whatever comes your way.

Now, you don't have to choose gratitude. You can choose another high American cultural value. It makes itself known when I shift responsibility away from my own actions and attitude to you. That's called blame.

How about a definition of gratitude—the quality of being thankful; readiness to show appreciation for and to return kindness.

How did you get here today? Well, you were born at a very early age. And since that time choices have been made. Not the least of which is that you signed your life away to the United States Government and the U.S. Army. Thank you, by the way.

But you made a choice. You did this to yourself.

I'm a marathon runner. Today is a rest day for me and I don't have a scheduled run. So, since it is a rest day, I inexplicably woke up before 0330. Not sure what that was about. I needed to get up at a reasonable time so we could arrive here by 0930 to set up and do final prep for this meal.

But, remember, today is a rest day. Tomorrow I'll get up before daylight to run my 21st consecutive Rock and Roll Nashville 26.2

AT THIS POINT

mile marathon. I'm a "Legacy Runner," which means I have done this to myself twenty years in a row, before now.

No one made me do it. I chose to do it.

I'm a little bummed. Since July a physical therapist and I have been working on an overwork injury. Not just to prepare me for this marathon, but to keep me as ready as I could be to hike 156 total miles I needed to do on three backpacking trips; one in August, September and October.

This injury, you see, I did to myself.

When our four kids were younger, we chose not to have chores. Now, we thought our kids needed to learn responsibility. Learning responsibility is a key to a resilient life. "Chores" are important. I just didn't like the word…chores. So we had a list. A list of things we get to do because we have a roof over our head and food to eat. Did you get that? A list of things we get to do because we have a roof over our head and food to eat.

Chores can be a chore. But to get to do something because we can, we get to—that may move us toward gratitude.

Gratitude takes root when I take responsibility for my actions and attitude. It grows when I consistently step toward "I get to" instead of "I have to" in daily life. I can choose to be grateful.

It's easier to be grateful when things are tracking like you want. You get the slot you want in school, the promotion below the zone you had hoped for, that "go" rather than a "no-go."

Some of you will pass this training and will graduate. You will be selected. Ahhh, but perhaps a trainer missed a mistake you made and you could hide a flaw in your character or skill. Or perhaps your skills aren't exactly where they need to be at this point. Learn from it. Humbly step toward this new reality.

Make the most of every opportunity.

AT THIS POINT

But it takes some growth in us all to have gratitude when it feels like the wheels are coming off.

For some of you, this training isn't or didn't go as well as you had hoped. You missed a critical skill. You have an underlying emotional, social, or professional issue that needs to be addressed.

Maybe you had a particularly bad day. Learn from it. Humbly step toward this new reality.

Make the most of every opportunity.

Sometimes we get what we deserve. Often, we get what we do not deserve.

You can make the most of every opportunity. You can choose—gratitude.

This will be only third Thanksgiving since I was born that I will not put my feet under my mama's table. Until my mama died that streak was fifty-six years. It's been a family priority and I'm privileged to have been able to do so. Wherever I've lived, in Tennessee or Kentucky or Chicago, I've been able to make it home for Thanksgiving. Now not every Christmas, or birthday, or anniversary. Some of those I've spent working. I've spent Christmas by myself.

For about the last five or so years of her life, my mama has had no idea who I was. My mama had dementia. In September of 2019 I sat by her side as she breathed her last breath and stepped into the presence of Jesus Christ.

Was I grateful for her condition? Not so much. But I have learned much because of it. The relationship with my mama was recently, well, not much of a relationship. Every once in a while, there was still a glimpse of who my mama once was. Just a glimpse, and it's gone.

AT THIS POINT

The real beauty at this point is looking back, reflecting on all those great years and some hard ones with my mama and daddy. Wonderful memories. Laughter. Joy. Disagreements that worked themselves out through love and hard words. Wow! I'm grateful for that legacy.

I watched my daddy, as he went through three bouts of cancer, care for the woman he loved as her memory slipped away. It was that third bout that took him out of this world.

I want the legacy of my family in the future to be an honorable one. On the one hand, I may need to be cared for in the future. On the other hand, it's what you do for those you love; you care for them, in gratitude.

Anyone can love someone who loves them back. The real challenge is to be able to love those who can't or don't love us. You know, like your enemy or the one whose stance in life seems hard and hurting.

I'm certainly not justifying abuse. Nope. In those cases, move straight to justice and, in time, forgiveness.

You don't have to be grateful for a specific event to gratefully learn from it.

In my faith tradition, I see examples of ugly turning out to be beauty.

A shepherd named David who was tapped to be King but did stupid by having an adulterous relationship with a woman who was not his wife and then he had her husband killed. And who said the Bible was boring? David was held accountable, found forgiveness and lived the consequences of those ugly choices the rest of his life.

But he encountered forgiveness.

AT THIS POINT

There is brutal honesty in the Psalms. Sometimes church people can gloss over the hard and ugly. But David shows his honesty with gratitude.

In my faith tradition, there was a death on a cross of just the right person at just the right time in history. It looked like the end, but it wasn't.

There are those who mature to the point in their lives where they can be grateful for hard and ugly events.

Gratitude is a bold step toward resilience.

I've had the privilege to share life and sit around a many a campfire with current serving military personnel. I've listened as they shared about people in their lives who have influenced them to be the people they are today. Some with admiration. Some with disdain.

Gratitude is not the avoidance of where you are or convincing yourself that the past didn't happen. It's looking it in the eye and seeing the glimmer of beauty in the ugly.

It's said that God doesn't waste anything. I don't think He wastes the hard or the hurtful.

Honestly, I want things like I want them, when I want them. That would make me honest, and human, and at times . . . selfish, and at times . . . foolish.

Maybe in the future, you'll be able to look back at a difficult, ugly, maybe even knee-buckling event and see that God met you right there. You found just the right attorney. This time the Chaplain's advice was right on the mark. Or your squad leader or commander's assignment was just what you needed though it was not what you wanted. And . . . it worked out in your best interest.

Sometimes it's difficult to be grateful when the circumstances of life are smoking you.

AT THIS POINT

I've walked this planet long enough to have knee-buckling challenges. This year my wife and I celebrated thirty-three years of marriage, and I will tell you there was a season when I wasn't sure that our marriage would last. Marriage is difficult. Relationships are difficult. Sometimes I'm difficult to live with. Sometimes she is. I stepped toward the help I needed. She stepped toward the help she needed. We stepped toward the help we needed.

The desire to be a person of character is to recognize truth and to move toward the reality of that. To say, this is where I am.

That person you asked to marry you isn't the problem. Or your squad leader or your Sergeant. Oh, they may have problems, but that just makes them imperfect humans, just like you. The problem is that it's hard, at times, to be grateful, at times, for the person you decided to walk some miles with.

It's hard so that probably means it's valuable.

I have friends who are my examples of how to do this well. I'm still working on it.

My opportunities are not yours. Your opportunities are not mine. What will you do with yours? Become a lifer? Be the first in your family to get a college degree?

But will you do it with gratitude? Because you don't have to, you get to.

We all need other voices in our lives that help us to adjust fire—correct our flight path and to move in a healthier direction.

There are those who know me really well, know my quirks, inconsistencies, hurt, and yet love me still. That says more about them than it does about me. And I am grateful.

Thank you for serving this country and watching my family's back on a global scale. Thank you for making it possible for me to

AT THIS POINT

put my feet under my mama's table for fifty-six previous years. I am a grateful man.

So today, and tomorrow, be grateful, thankful for where you are and what you've chosen to step toward.

I have a challenge for you. Make the most of every opportunity and step toward gratitude. Step toward a grateful look where you are now, where you have been, and where you want to go.

AT THIS POINT

 January 20, 2022
Grief

> He is despised and rejected of men, a Man of sorrows, and acquainted with grief. (Isaiah 53:3 NKJV)

It's the unwanted cousin who shows up at the most inopportune time and rattles the frame of my life to its foundations.

Have you heard people say, "Good grief?" I have. Probably said it myself. I think that's a misnomer.

Somewhat.

There was a young Soldier on a recent retreat with the last name of Grief. His name gave me pause. I suspect that's a last name that wasn't easy growing up with. I can think of a few names that are far worse. I don't recall him being a "grief."

My mama told me after her own mother died she would think about her at the oddest times. It was a smell, an image, or an event that brought the memories back. She was right.

The day after my parents' funerals were tough days. I figured out how tired I was, the weight of the days before and after. Neither of my parents are in this world now. They have moved on to the next one, a new one, a far better one. I still miss them.

Grief takes up residence when I realize that I have an expectation in an unrealistic reality. Somehow a thought moved in my head that this person I love and who means so much to me will somehow live forever on this earth. How's that for an errant thought?

AT THIS POINT

But they won't. We all know it. Even with very clear evidence to the contrary, it's hard to convince myself until I must.

Even though we know it to be true, it still sneaks up on us. Tears flow. Hope wanes. I mourn.

Grief is that unsettling uncertainty that "I missed it": an event, an opportunity, a trend, a decision with far reaching consequences while being focused on something else I thought was important. It is bumping into my own humanness that I cannot manage all the complicated relationships of life as well as I thought, I hoped.

It's loss. Yet another addition in the house of unrealized expectations.

We all know grief doesn't just visit when someone dies. Yes, people we love do die. And those we love make seemingly irreparable decisions from which they may never return.

I too make decisions that profoundly affect those around me which can adversely change their lives.

Right in the middle of so many things that are going so very well, there is this one thing that somehow destabilizes everything and sucks the life out of me. It's a reminder that what might have been, may not be. An overwhelming sense that what could have been, what I had hoped might be, will not be.

Grief debilitates. Deep grief forces me to decide if I will pick up one foot and put it in front of the other. The inhospitable reminder that my foundation can't be set in the temporal.

And yet, I am not alone. Grief is not new. Perhaps my residence in it is. And then, periodically, it keeps showing up from time to time.

There is hope in this life and there is hope for the next. Yet, I nor anyone else gets to make any more choices after we step from this life to the next. There is no do over.

AT THIS POINT

I have a friend whose daughter has made choices that are incongruent with the values she was taught that even the daughter espoused while she was growing up. We were talking about this one we both love, and her mother said, "As long as she's living, there's hope."

There it is.

Oh, how I like directness that is solidly grounded. I cling to the same hope for my own kids, and maybe myself too.

At this point I'll realign my thinking on the sure foundation of life in Christ. I'll paint the walls of my house with sadness and tears. I'll grieve. And I'll place my hope in the One who knows how human I am and is acquainted with grief.

"Out of the depths I cry to you, LORD; Lord, hear my voice. Let your ears be attentive to my cry for mercy." (Psalm 130:1,2)

AT THIS POINT

BENCHMARK History and Foundations
Part 3

Some people may be curious about how, when, and why this nonprofit called BENCHMARK Adventure Ministries began. Here you will bump into the core values and foundational concepts on which this organization began and which still guide all we do.

AT THIS POINT

This is the first letter I wrote about BENCHMARK Adventure Ministries. I chuckle that it was originally in dot matrix and is three pages long. Probably only three people, including my parents, could have made it all the way through. This is the original letter, as is. It's what happens when I didn't have a good editor 30 years ago. It's followed by the same text for ease of reading. – J.H.E.

AT THIS POINT

April 17, 1993

An open letter to friends,

I don't know why it is, but I have a difficult time sitting down and writing. Writing in my journal, writing reports, writing those articles for which I have concepts, writing letters. Perhaps it is tied to the deeply held idea that to do is better than just being. So I do the most obvious needed things.

Do understand that I have for the last six or so years struggled against this doing perfectionist mindset, but it lingers. I will probably struggle against this part of the old man for years to come, and struggle I will.

I settled into my quiet time and read my daily Chamber's selection from My Utmost for His Highest. Then I was going to journal. If you have Chamber's for today's date, ... well I was prompted to do something a little different. My journaling would take a different form. I would write a letter. There are several people which I have needed and wanted to write, but I have allowed other things to crowd that task out. I so enjoy receiving notes and I have an understanding of the cost of time and mental energy. But, I just don't do it.

As I look at my DayTimers I see that my time here in Nashville is short. My first High Road trip with Wheaton College is just three weeks away. The Lord willing, in 21 days I will be in the North Woods of Wisconsin anticipating and making final plans for my first students of the summer (my summer starts early). As I look forward, I get reflective. What have I accomplished since my last trip in August? What have I learned?

I have been desiring to get involved in full time vocational ministry, so last summer I applied to the Nashville Union Mission having heard of a possible opening. I visited several times, considered the possibilities and had to turn it down. The choices I have felt God directing me in have not been the easiest. I wanted the job. I was weary of being asked what I did and not being able to say that I was directly using my education. Ken Kalisch (High Road Program Manager) and I talked and if I would have taken the job I would have taken it for the wrong reason. I wanted to be able to say, "I work for the Union Mission". Or I work somewhere interesting. But I could not. I have always known the peace of God even in tough decisions and I just did not have it relative to this choice.

So instead of trying to stabilize an image for myself through a job, Barbara and I decided that I would not work at all and apply myself to several other tasks. I became a house husband. The change from the culturally correct bread winner to primary non earner was not easy either. My self image, like the general male population, is so tied to what I do. God had ordered my steps so that I could begin dealing with that mis-aligned part of my life head on.

I heighten my look to find places to get involved. September thru Mid October I put a lot of energy into directing a Fall youth retreat for the Cumberland Association. I gathered a volunteer staff of five people who had not been that involved in past retreats and we developed an objective driven retreat. I say that like it is something new. Well, it is. Most retreats and conferences are a lot of activities with a theme for the presented material. I wanted the whole retreat to be consistently in line with the objectives. We dealt with Matthew 6:25-33 and called it "First Things First". I was able to share my knowledge and skill in a wonderful teaching situation while carrying out an important ministry function. The retreat went very well. Many good comments from teens and adults. It was cohesive in purpose and specific in content. It was a great chance to be an educator.

In the fall I also audited Systematic Theology under F. Leroy Forlines. It was great fun. Yes, a theology class can be great fun. I also participated in group discussions. My mind was stretched, I was able to clarify some ideas and the content was stimulating. I have used ideas clarified in that class in four youth lessons on Spiritual Disciplines for Randall House I wrote in the fall and in a 6 week study of free will and

AT THIS POINT

election study which I am now doing in the Senior High Sunday School class I teach. What fun it is to be an educator.

Between Christmas and New Years I participated in the State Youth Conference in Gatlinberg, TN where I was a chaperone and a seminar elective leader. I presented material to the few who attended my seminar on journaling as a spiritual discipline. It went well.

In the fall, I did a lot of gardening, both in my own yard and others. Barbara has always wanted to plant flowers and have vegetable garden. It is happening. We have a 14 X 16 foot flower plot with three types of daffodils, Blue-eyed Mary, Hyacinths, Anemones and Chionodoxa. Much of that was planted as bulbs last October. That doesn't count the nandina, forsythia, a dogwood, a tulip poplar, a red maple, and clematis I have moved in. Now that it is spring, we have tulips blooming and iris on the way.

We have put in a small vegetable garden this spring with spinach, lettuce, onions, carrots, radishes, several herbs, corn, tomatoes, zucchini, peas, sunflower for the birds, broccoli and bell peppers.

The winter months were not as productive as I would have liked. Not as much to be "active" in. The day after Thanksgiving while doing some work for my parents in Georgia I hurt my lower back. I thought it would go away. It did not. So, I went to an orthopedic surgeon and was told I had a swollen disc. I spend several weeks going to a sports medicine therapist and doing stretching and strengthening exercises. The last four months I have been going to a fitness center 3 days a week trying to get healthy before summer (May 7th). I am pleased to say that I am physically stronger but still having some discomfort in my lower back. At the age of thirty, I am even developing a small chest. Time will tell how I do. Prayer would help too.

Another thing that came out of the winter happened while having lunch with Mark McPeak, a minister of our church. He asked if I had ever considered developing seminars and leading trips on my own. He was very encouraging. I told him that I really appreciated him telling me of the gifts he had seen in me. Since I was not "at work, vocationally" in ministry and not being really sure but very curious about where God was leading me, it was nice to hear someone say he saw some potential. If not in one area, maybe another. Perhaps I had been lured into indecision by the passing of time. I have been involved constantly since college in education, but I have had no clear idea where it was taking me. I was walking by faith, be grudgingly at times.

After some additional prayer and some discussions with Barbara, we have decided to develop a business ministry to challenge people in whole life change. I say we because she is the financial backing and I am developing a name, a brochure and other ideas more formally. These things have been in my head for several years, it now seems like this is the time to take another step of faith. Since talking with a few people about personal spiritual growth through small group problem solving and task accomplishment, I have received only encouragement. I will have an exhibit at the National Youth Conference of Free Will Baptist. It could be an interesting year.

The ministry will have three sides. First, I will develop an intensive 48 hour activity based weekend program of challenges for the whole person which will be applicable to youth groups, deacon boards, prospective missionaries, state and national board members, church staffs both professional and volunteer; any group of people who desire to learn a little more about how they function in small group situations. This is a practical way to learn and apply Biblical principles to daily life.

Second will be a seminar side. With a lower level of activity but with the same emphasis of applying Biblical principles to everyday living and ministry situations. Personal disciplines of the faith can be stressed as well as including active, participatory elements to teaching situations.

The third side is a wilderness tripping program. Trips of five - seven days and longer will be planned to provide people with an intense learning situation. Backpacking and/or canoeing will be the means of

AT THIS POINT

travel. The setting could include the Savage Gulf area of Tennessee, the Great Smoky Mountains and the Big South Fork National Parks, and during June into the Upper Peninsula of Michigan and along Lake Superior. There is also the potential for trips to be planned into the Boundary Waters Canoe Area, the Adirondacks and the Colorado Rockies.

The name may be BENCHMARK Adventure Ministries. On a topographical map a benchmark is a equilateral triangle with a small dot in the center. If a person knows a little about maps this can be a place you can get your bearings. A Benchmark is a known point. They can be used to determine your relationship to another point or goal. There are several parallels between the topographical benchmark and what I will be trying to do with this ministry. The ministry thrust will be three sided. The attempt will be to challenge and minister to the whole person; 1. Mind, 2. Heart, and 3. Will. Or to challenge the way a person thinks, feels and acts. The dot in the middle will show the value of a Christ centered and Biblically based view of living life and how that emphasis affects the whole of our being.

Last fall my pastor and I took a two day backpacking trip together. We hiked and talked and then I helped him to abseil for his first time. Abseiling is what many also know as rappelling. (Thought you needed to learn a new word). He had a good time and was able to glean some sermon illustrations from our outing. On the trip back, he wanted to know if I would take all the church staff on such a trip in the spring. Next week a group of 6 should be bantering around together for a time of retreat; no watches and no telephones. (April 22, 23)

Most recently I have been working at Hillmont Camp 3 days a week since March 22nd. I have been developing some program elements that the maintenance staff may not have gotten to before summer. Some of what I have done is to build a new 12 foot wall in the challenge course, developed two 9 hole disc (frisbee) golf courses, developed an archery area, more clearly defined horseshoe area in two camp areas, and put in some permanent benches.

March 29th I began a Red Cross Lifeguard Class to become a certified lifeguard. My advanced lifesaving certification had lapsed and felt I needed to improve my skills before a new summer of wilderness trips. The certification is very important considering I will be seeking to lead my own trips. My final exam including the physical skills is next week. The question is "Can I tread water for one minute while holding a ten pound weight out of the water?" The answer, I must if I am to be certified.

So after all this, now what?

I feel the pressure to get all my personal ends tied up so that I can concentrate on this first course. Little projects that have to be done, ministry responsibilities pasted off to someone else, things around the house taken care of and getting mentally ready to be Senior Instructor for another summer of trips. The days are passing more rapidly than the tasks are getting done.

Well, that sort of catches a person up to present. Take a chance to drop me a note in return. Just acknowledge the effort of the perfectionists doer and this effort at being still and reflecting.

This has been just the facts. But rest assured that I am a bit anxious that I use my time well up to the time of the trip. I need to continue to be before God especially in the last days and that my physical hindrances will be minimized by His strength in me.

Because of Christ in me,

James H. Evans

AT THIS POINT

April 17, 1993

An open letter to friends.

I don't know why it is, but I have a difficult time sitting down and writing. Writing in my journal, writing reports, writing those articles for which I have concepts, writing letters. Perhaps it is tied to the deeply held idea that to do is better than just being. So I do the most obvious needed things.

Do understand that I have for the last six or so years struggled against this doing perfectionist mindset, but it lingers. I will probably struggle against this part of the old man for years to come, and struggle I will.

I settled into my quiet time and read my daily Chamber's selection from My Upmost for His Highest. Then I was going to journal. If you have Chamber's for today's date... well I was prompted to do something a little different. My journaling would take a different form, I would write a letter. There are several people which I have needed and wanted to write, but I have allowed other things to crowd that task out. I so enjoy receiving notes and I have an understanding of the cost of time and mental energy. But, I just don't do it.

As I look at my DayTimers I see that my time here in Nashville is short. My first High Road trip with Wheaton College is just three weeks away. The Lord willing, in 21 days I will be in the North Woods of Wisconsin anticipating and making final plans for my first students of the summer (my summer starts early). As I look

AT THIS POINT

forward, I get reflective. What have I accomplished since my last trip in August? What have I learned?

I have been desiring to get involved in full-time vocational ministry, so last summer I applied to the Nashville Union Mission having heard of a possible opening. I visited several times, considered the possibilities and had to turn it down. The choices I have felt God directing me have not been the easiest. I wanted the job, I was weary of being asked what I did and not being able to say that I was directly using my education. Ken Kalisch (High Road Program Manager) and I talked and if I would have taken the job I would have taken it for the wrong reason. I wanted to be able to say, "I work for the Union Mission". Or I work somewhere interesting. But I could not. I have always known the peace of God even in tough decisions and I just did not have it relative to this choice.

So instead of trying to stabilize an image for myself through a job, Barbara and I decided that I would not work at all and apply myself to several other tasks. I became a house husband. The change from the culturally correct breadwinner to primary non-earner was not easy either. My self-image, like the general male population, is so tied to what I do. God had ordered my steps so that I could begin dealing with that misaligned part of my life head on.

I heightened my look to find places to get involved. September thru Mid October I put a lot of energy into directing a Fall youth retreat for the Cumberland Association. I gathered a volunteer staff of five people who had not been that involved in past retreats and we developed an objective driven retreat. I say that like it is

AT THIS POINT

something new. Well, it is. Most retreats and conferences are a lot of activities with a theme for the presented material. I wanted the whole retreat to be consistently in line with the objectives. We dealt with Matthew 6:25–33 and called it "First Things First". I was able to share my knowledge and skill in a wonderful teaching situation while carrying out an important ministry function. The retreat went very well. Many good comments from teens and adults. It was cohesive in purpose and specific in contact. It was a great chance to be an educator.

In the fall I also audited systematic theology under F. Leroy Forlines. It was great fun. Yes, a theology class can be great fun. I also participated in group discussions. My mind was stretched, I was able to clarify some ideas and the contact was stimulating. I have used ideas clarified in that class in four youth lessons on Spiritual Disciplines for Randall House I wrote in the fall and in a 6 week study of free will and election study which I am now doing in the Senior High Sunday School class I teach. What fun it is to be an educator.

Between Christmas and New Years I participated in the State Youth Conference in Gatlinburg, TN where I was a chaperone and a seminar elective leader. I presented material to the few who attended my seminar on journaling as a spiritual discipline. It went well.

In the fall, I did a lot of gardening, both in my own yard and others. Barbara has always wanted to plant flowers and have vegetable garden. It is happening. We have a 14 X 16 foot flower plot with three types of daffodils, Blue-eyed mary, Hyacinths, Anemones

AT THIS POINT

and Chionodoxa. Much of that was planted as bulbs last October. That doesn't count the nandina, forsythia, a dogwood, a tulip poplar, red maple, and clematis I have moved in. Now that it is spring, we have tulips and blooming and iris on the way.

We have put in a small vegetable garden this spring with spinach, lettuce, onions, carrots, radishes, several herbs, corn, tomatoes, zucchini, peas, sunflower for the birds, broccoli and bell peppers.

The winter months were not as productive as I would have liked. Not as much to be "active" in. The day after Thanksgiving while doing some work for my parents and Georgia I hurt my lower back. I thought it would go away. It did not. So, I went to an orthopedic surgeon and was told I had a swollen disc. I spend several weeks going to a sports medicine therapist and doing stretching and strengthening exercises. The last four months I have been going to a fitness center three days a week trying to get healthy before the summer (May 7th). I am pleased to say that I am physically stronger but still having some discomfort in my lower back. At the age of thirty, I am even developing a small chest. Time will tell how I do. Prayer would help too.

Another thing that came out of the winter happened while having lunch with Mark McPeak, a minister of our church. He asked if I had ever considered developing seminars and leading trips on my own. He was very encouraging. I told him that I really appreciated him telling me of the gifts he had seen in me. Since I was not "at work vocationally" in ministry and not really being sure but very curious about where God was leading me, it was nice to hear someone say he saw some potential. If not in one area, maybe

AT THIS POINT

another. Perhaps I have been lured into indecision by the passing of time. I have been involved constantly since college in education, but I have had no clear idea where it was taking me. I was walking by faith, begrudgingly at times.

After some additional prayer and some discussions with Barbara, we have decided to develop a business ministry to challenge people toward whole life change. I say we because she is the financial backing and I am developing a name, a brochure and other ideas more formally. These things have been in my head for several years, it now seems like this is the time to take another step of faith. Since talking with a few people about personal spiritual growth through small group problem solving and task accomplishment, I have received only encouragement. I will have an exhibit at the National Youth Conference of Free Will Baptist. It could be an interesting year.

The ministry will have three sides. First I will develop an intensive 48 hour activity based weekend program of challenges for the whole person which will be applicable to youth groups, deacon boards, prospective missionaries, state and national board members, church staffs both professional and volunteer; any group of people who desire to learn a little more about how they function in small group situations. This is a practical way to learn and apply Biblical principles to daily life.

Second will be a seminar side. With a lower level of activity but with the same emphasis of applying Biblical principles to everyday living and ministry situations. Personal disciplines of the faith can

AT THIS POINT

be stressed as well as including active, participatory elements to teaching situations.

The third side is a wilderness tripping program. Trips of five - seven days and longer will be planned to provide people with an intense learning situation. Backpacking and / or canoeing will be the means of travel. The setting could include the Savage Gulf area of Tennessee, the Great Smoky Mountains and the Big South Fork National Parks, and during June into the Upper Peninsula of Michigan and along Lake Superior. There is also the potential for trips to be planned into the Boundary Waters Canoe Area, the Adirondacks and the Colorado Rockies.

The name may be BENCHMARK Adventure Ministries. On a topographical map a benchmark is an equilateral triangle with a small dot in the center. If a person knows a little about maps this can be a place you can get your bearings. A Benchmark is a known point. They can be used to determine your relationship to another point or goal. There are several parallels between the topographical benchmark and what I will be trying to do with this ministry. The ministry thrust will be three sided. The attempt will be to challenge and minister to the whole person; 1. Mind, 2. Heart, and 3. Will. Or to challenge the way a person thinks, feels, and acts. The dot in the middle will show the value of a Christ centered and Biblically based view of living life and how that emphasis affects the whole of our being.

Last fall my pastor and I took a two-day backpacking trip together. We hiked and talked and then I helped him to abseil for the first time. Abseiling is what many know as reppelling. (Thought you

AT THIS POINT

needed to learn a new word). He had a good time and was able to glean some sermon illustrations from our outing. On the trip back, he wanted to know if I would take all the church stuff on such a trip in the spring. Next week a group of 6 should be bantering around together for a time of retreat; no watches and no telephones. (April 22, 23)

Most recently I have been working at Hillmont Camp 3 days a week since March 22. I have been developing some program elements that the maintenance staff may have not gotten to before summer. Some of what I have done is to build a new 12 foot wall and the challenge course, developed two 9-hole disc (frisbee) golf courses, developed an archery area, more clearly defined horseshoe area in two camp areas, and put in some permanent benches.

March 29th I began a Red Cross Lifeguard Class to become a certified lifeguard. My advanced life saving certification had lapsed and felt I needed to improve my skills before a new summer of wilderness trips. The certification is very important considering I will be seeking to lead my own trips. My final exam, including the physical skills, is next week. The question is "Can I tread water for one minute while holding a ten-pound weight out of the water?" The answer, I must if I am to be certified.
So after all this, now what?

I feel the pressure to get all of my personal ends tied up so that I can concentrate on this first course. Little projects that have to be done, ministry responsibilities passed off to someone else, things around the house taking care of and getting mentally ready to be

AT THIS POINT

a Senior Instructor for another summer of trips. The days are passing more rapidly than the tasks are getting done.

Well, that sort of catches a person up to present. Take a chance to drop me a note in return. Just acknowledge the effort of the perfectionists-doer and this effort at being still and reflecting.

This has just been the facts. But, rest assured that I am a bit anxious that I use my time well up to the time of the trip. I need to continue to be before God especially in the last days and that my physical hindrances will be minimized by His strength in me.

Because of Christ in me;

James H. Evans

AT THIS POINT

What's a benchmark?

benchmark, a surveyor's mark made on a permanent landmark that has a known position and altitude: benchmarks are used as reference points ...
– Webster's New Universal Unabridged Dictionary

Why BENCHMARK? It's not because we think this ministry is the standard by which all others should be measured, which is a common usage of the word.

Our name is taken from a topographic map symbol, a benchmark, an equilateral triangle with a small mark in the center. Whether in the wilderness or in the city, a benchmark is a known point, a permanent point of reference, which can help us better understand exactly where we are, almost anywhere in the world.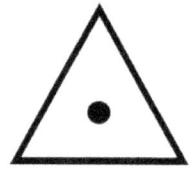

In a physical location the United States Geological Survey (USGS) installs a simple metal disc set in stone inscribed with a triangle and a small mark in the center. A benchmark has two planes: vertical and horizontal. In this country, the USGS determines the location of each specific benchmark and its relationships to other features like roads, streams, or mountains. That's the horizontal plane. Vertically, the USGA confirms its elevation in relation to sea level, another known point.

BENCHMARK Adventure Ministries designs interactive experiences and outdoor adventures to help individuals assess their horizontal relationship with other people, their surroundings and Creation, and their vertical relationship with God. The small mark in the middle of the triangle symbolizes the high value of a

AT THIS POINT

Christ centered, Biblical worldview and how that emphasis affects the whole person. The three sides of the triangle represent BENCHMARK's focus on the whole person: the mind, the heart, and the will utilizing the program elements of seminars, retreats and wilderness trips.

A BENCHMARK experience helps you to better understand where you are and will challenge you to evaluate the way you think, feel, and act in light of Biblical principles.

The mission of BENCHMARK Adventure Ministries is to stimulate significant life change toward wholeness in Christ through interactive experiences and outdoor adventures.

AT THIS POINT

Frustrating People for 25 Years, March 15, 2018

The Founder's address during the 25th Anniversary Celebration of BENCHMARK. The dinner committee gave 10 minutes to talk about 25 years of ministry. My first thought, "That's all?" So, with 24 seconds per year, here it goes. Please pardon the repetition.

Good evening. As the Founder of BENCHMARK Adventure Ministries, thank you so much for coming to BENCHMARK's 25th Anniversary Celebration. I sincerely appreciate your decision to be here tonight, from just a few minutes away to several hours down the road, from Ohio, Minnesota, even Lilburn, Georgia.

Tonight, I find myself a little overwhelmed. My mind is racing through so many people who have made and are making BENCHMARK Adventure Ministries what it is.

In the 1990s I led sixteen 16-19-day wilderness trips, taught high school Sunday school, served on a church committee, and led retreats with a couple of camps in Middle Tennessee. In 1992 my wife Barbara and I had been married 5 years. That same year, Mark McPeak was the adult pastor of the church we attended at the time. He encouraged the gifts he saw in me and used his considerable abilities to move BENCHMARK forward. It was Mark who wrote BENCHMARK's appeal letter for our very first Backpack for BENCHMARK in 1995 and fifty people donated.

I think of Vicky Smith and Barbara who for years encouraged me, and along with Mark McPeak became BENCHMARK's

AT THIS POINT

Advisory Board in early 1994. Those three people served a combined total of fifty-two years as Board members. Later that year Jim Lauthern joined us. I could list the other eighteen men and women who have served on the BENCHMARK Board. I'm so very grateful.

But if I listed the men and women who served as board members, staff, volunteers or those hundreds of organizational leaders who allowed BENCHMARK to have a part of their on-going work, it would sound like one of those biblical genealogies and you'd stop listening.

But just like a seemingly boring biblical genealogy, there is such richness in God's grace that's worth acknowledging.

On March 15, 1993, "it" began. When "it" started, "it" didn't have a name.

By that summer a name was determined and BENCHMARK had its first retreat near College Station, Texas, with fifty high schoolers in the fall. We were mobile. Over the next year corporation papers were submitted, excess medical coverage for participants obtained, Federal Employer Identification Number assigned, and IRS 501(c)(3) nonprofit status applied for and gained by snail mail. The State of Tennessee Corporation papers are stamped 14 MAR 94.

While preparing for those long wilderness trips, my assistant and I would spend days talking about how we thought God was involved in our lives and what we were learning as a result. With that awareness and the pre-course reading in mind, we'd develop the objections that would shape our entire trip.

Because this northern Wisconsin/Upper Peninsula of Michigan-based wilderness program was Wheaton College's Northwood Campus, the adult courses had college or graduate school

AT THIS POINT

academic requirements culminating in a three-to-five-page reflection paper submitted a month after the trip. As I compared the content of the student papers to each other, it would appear as if all these students and I were on different trips. The themes they wrote about were so different from the theme my assistant and I had taught.

But God was doing so much more.

While we worked to develop our objectives through adventure and instruction, God was using our efforts to tailor-design the educational experience to each person. It was beautiful. It's as if God was saying "Trust me. Life is wonderful and fun, and hard and challenging. Trust me. I'll walk through it with you. When others leave, I am here. Watch me do something that will be difficult for you to explain."

Those lessons from the 1990s still guide me today.

From BENCHMARK's very first high school youth retreat in Texas, to serving annually a group of sixth graders through team building from a local church for twenty years to US Military big Army and Special Operations units to Men of Valor just this past Thursday, there is quite the wonderful variety in the groups we serve. We've served over 13,000 participants through 434 ministry events in twenty-five years.

You know that we all live in a world with relational brokenness, disconnection and loss. And I know that the pressures of this life can squeeze out hope for my own family, maybe yours too. BENCHMARK Adventure Ministries comes alongside our ministry partners by creating adventure events for relational connection and personal reflection.

AT THIS POINT

Adventure is all about meeting people where they are, taking them beyond where they think they want to go, and leading them where they need to be.

There have been seasons when I have questioned the decision to start a nonprofit and had days when I didn't think BENCHMARK would make it to the end of the year. God has been faithful. So many people have been kind and faithful. I see God working it out in me over time and He is good. He's working His best out in others too.

BENCHMARK is a little unorthodox. I've been called crazy so many times that I thought it was becoming my middle name. But I'm not . . . crazy. And Jesus is unorthodox and I only want Him to smile.

On Thursday of this week, BENCHMARK staff led twenty-one clients and staff men from Men of Valor on a day of climbing and rappelling. All their clients have been previously incarcerated. The sixty-six-year-old man I rode with had spent twenty-four years in prison for something he did and most recently spent twenty-nine months in prison for a crime he did not commit. BENCHMARK's task was to take them on an adventure, to be who we are in Christ, to serve well, to be all there. Their Discipleship Director happily told me that they can really build off the day to serve their men.

It's not magic. It's a willingness to have a small part in a person's life, in their journey to Christ or with Christ. To be all in for however long the paths cross . . . and then to leave the results to God. What I hear Him saying is, "Trust me, I'm God, I'm a better teacher that you are. Do you want those you serve to know you or know Me?"

This journey called BENCHMARK has been a personal one and is intertwined with my life and my family. On the one hand, I'm

AT THIS POINT

kinda normal. I have a wife of thirty years who is a labor and delivery nurse and nurse educator. We are still raising four kids who have been taught in public schools; three of them have graduated high school. My kids have never known a time that BENCHMARK wasn't a part of our lives.

I'm also a little different than some. I'm not an adrenaline junky or an adventure junky.

But I do know that discomfort and pain are great teachers, that the adventure of life is used by God to draw us to Himself and to help us grow, change, mature. I didn't say it was all fun.

I enjoy the outdoors, value it, steward it, and have been trained by it. I don't love it. I love the God whose creativity it embodies, even the harsh and seemingly ugly.

Though I enjoy air conditioning and a roof over my head, I want to live life saying, "Come on, let's go," instead of life saying "You go on without me."

I simply wanted to use whatever capabilities and inabilities I have to serve. I want to be a part of enticing people to join a journey and to follow Christ wherever in the world it takes them. People who, no matter their occupation, make it their life's work to serve others for Christ and His Kingdom.

You see, I've been in entirely too many settings where people were trying to teach something eternally significant in an uninteresting way.

Our interactive experiences and outdoor adventures create a setting for all involved to consider how they're currently living with an eye toward being different, better, healthier, mature, complete in Christ. One decision today can completely change life.

Oh yes, I've made a lot of relational mistakes. I've hurt others and been hurt too. There was a time when I was ready to quit this

AT THIS POINT

journey and needed someone to tell me that my life and the ministry I was doing was valuable, helpful, and significant. Other times I needed to simply believe the God I say I serve and trust Him even more.

Growth is hard, good, and uncomfortable.

Today our values are still as important as when BENCHMARK began. They still provide a framework we aspire to and embody:

- Spiritual formation and leadership development for all involved; participants, staff, volunteers and founder.
- Commitment to be a debt-free ministry.
- Seeking strategic involvement, trusting God with the results.
- Speaking the truth, desiring to do so in love.
- Acting in others' best interest.
- Making the most of every opportunity.

BENCHMARK has always been about people, not an organizational structure or location. The themes of pilgrim and aliens in the Bible remind me I nor you will be on this planet long.

You see, I know that the God I serve is especially good working in and through the imperfect and hardheaded. What brings a smile is that by the grace of God, the generosity of donors and volunteers, and a bit of hardheadedness, this experiment called BENCHMARK Adventure Ministries continues.

Celebrate with us today. Our mission is to stimulate significant life change toward wholeness in Christ. That...THAT makes getting up every day worth it.

AT THIS POINT

Near the beginning of the world-wide pandemic, this was sent during regular monthly email communication as a Ministry Update from James H Evans, Founder.

April 27, 2020
We're OK

I am doing well and I hope you are too. If you're not, and need to talk to someone, reply to this email with your prayer concern or call my cell.

A significant amount of our ministry is focused on our Chaplains Partnership Initiative, coming alongside Chaplains to serve them and the Soldiers and Families they serve. On Saturday, April 18th, the Pentagon communicated that it would extend its ban on most military and domestic travel until June 30th.[1] This will significantly limit our face-to-face service for the next two months.

Until we are able to continue our adventure ministry events, we don't push pause on our purpose. Our mission to stimulate significant life change toward wholeness in Christ continues.

- Contact is being maintained with Chaplains and Religious Affairs Specialists who, like we, are figuring out how to have a ministry of presence without being present. Some are looking toward potential August or September ministry events.
- BENCHMARK is in the final steps of a migration/integration to streamline office systems.

AT THIS POINT

- Time is being blocked out to write lessons learned and the teaching content that's shaped thirty years of ministry.

While this ministry has ongoing needs, our regular and monthly donors, including some who sent recent unexpected gifts, are sustaining us. Because of those who stand with us through prayer and financial contributions, we are doing well. I am thankful to you and to God who provides.

Your donations are being wisely stewarded. We are free of any long-term debt since 1993. Expenses are reduced. Designated and additional funds are being held in reserve so BENCHMARK can say "yes" to ministry events as soon as it is wise to do so. We stand ready to partner with previous and new ministry partners.

If you want to make an immediate financial impact, perhaps donating to one of our ministry partners is a good choice: Donelson Christian Academy, Men of Valor, or One Generation Away.

AT THIS POINT

July 2022

Ask the Founder, almost anything, about BENCHMARK Adventure Ministries
2022 Forging Resilience Dinner Questions

Do you do any events partnered with groups outside the military? – M. Wanca

Historically we have done more events in the past than in recent years. BENCHMARK leads our own signature events; Appalachian Trail Outreach and the Chuck Wilson Memorial Backpack for BENCHMARK. In the last three years we have served Brentwood United Methodist Church fifth graders, Donelson Christian Academy, City of Shakopee, Minnesota, Men of Valor, First Southern Methodist Church, and True Core Academy. We remain available to serve church, school, nonprofit and corporate groups.

How many states/countries has BENCHMARK ministered in?

Two countries; United States and Mexico

Twelve states plus Washington, DC: Georgia, Florida, Illinois, Kentucky, Minnesota, North Carolina, South Carolina, Tennessee, Texas, Virginia, Washington, and Washington, DC.

Through our Chaplains Partnership Initiative we primarily serve units from Fort Campbell, Kentucky; Fort Benning, Georgia;

AT THIS POINT

Hunter Army Airfield, Georgia; Joint Base Lewis-McChord, Washington; Fort Jackson, South Carolina; Fort Bragg, North Carolina.

Over the years, how many nights have you slept on the ground, on average?

I have no idea. More than some. Less than others. Do I really have to count them? Our ministry events put us sleeping on the ground, at retreat and conference centers, and in hotels. We're mobile. No telling where we'll sleep.

Do you also work with women? All the videos are with men. – M. Leedy
Do lady soldiers attend events?
Is there a women's ministry focus in BENCHMARK? – E. Israel-Grover

We do serve women. We do have ministry events that female Soldiers and female children of Soldiers participate in.

As of 2020, there were 74,592 total women on active duty in the U.S. Army, with 16,987 serving as officers and 57,605 enlisted. While the Army has the highest number of total active-duty members, the ratio of women-men is lower than the U.S. Air Force and the U.S. Navy, with women making up 15.5% of total active-duty Army in 2020.

By percentages, we'll serve more males than females.

Though most of the units we serve are mostly male, we regularly have females on our ministry events. Males and females serve together in their military units, so we serve them together. If an opportunity develops and we have exclusively female leadership to lead a female only event, BENCHMARK will happily step toward that opportunity.

AT THIS POINT

From how many different states do you find active volunteers? – S. Clinton

Not as many as we would like. In the last three years, staff and volunteers have come from Georgia, Florida, Kentucky, Tennessee, Massachusetts, North Carolina, and Ohio.

Marathons – wow! When are you going to start doing Ironman Triathlon? – G. McLane

I don't currently plan to do an Ironman. I don't have ready access to a pool and it's not something I have interest in making time to do. A marathon is enough distance for me to be challenged, to keep me training through the winter months, and helps me to maintain an adequate physical fitness. I'll leave the Ironman to real athletes.

How do you know when to rest? Do you fight it or feel guilty? (You shouldn't)

Nightly sleep is a priority for me. Sleep is magical. I like to work, and I like this work. Our ministry events can have full days. The words of my daddy come to mind; "It doesn't take long to spend the night around here."

Resting my mind, body, and spirit helps me to be ready for the next day's demands. It's very possible to work and rest at the same time. Though backpacking, hiking, canoeing, and kayaking can be demanding, it is rest for my mind and spirit. I am a fan of short naps.

AT THIS POINT

Is there any way to make camping more comfortable? – H. Sanchez

Equipment has improved over the years and it helps. Being in creation necessitates being uncomfortable at times. Cold and wet isn't my favorite. Too hot and dry can be unfun too. But it's good for us to be uncomfortable.

Buy the best equipment you can afford to get started.

I try to keep my eye on the potential benefits: exploring Creation, developing shared memories, learning to be content with what I have, and being reminded that what I experience while camping far exceeds watching other people do something.

What is the best way to thaw a chicken in the backcountry? – L. Joseph

Warmth over time is the short answer. The longer answer is planning ahead to take advantage of warmth over time in a fluid environment without getting it too warm too soon for the weather conditions which creates other significantly worse problems.

Ahhh, Louis, you know every possible way we tried on that retreat.

What is your favorite Disney memory? – Walt Disney

Our entire family of six went to the Florida Disney Parks in 2013.

In my upcoming book called At This Point I use an exchange between the witch doctor baboon and the future king to illustrate the value of reflection. Rafiki describes running from the past or learning from it. Good words.

Periodically I have the powerful voice of Idina Menzel from "Frozen" fame stuck in my head. I keep trying to "Let It Go" but

AT THIS POINT

it's still there from time to time. This question brought it back again.

Is there a succession plan?
A succession plan was developed and approved by the Board of Directors in 2018 with the Founder's input, defining a process to be implemented if the Executive Director unexpectedly steps off the scene. In the future there will be a successor; however, that successor hasn't been found and currently is not needed.

What are the three Rs?
Responsibility, personal
    This is where I am
    The present
Reflection
    This is where I've been
    The past
Refocus
    This is where I need to go
    The Future

Develop your own "I need to remember…" statement

My next best step is…

AT THIS POINT

What is the most dangerous or death-defying experience you had during a retreat? – T. Moore
Tell us the most severe or unusual injury you have suffered on a BENCHMARK adventure. – J. Calton

Dangerous or death-defying experience? Driving to a ministry event. Have you been on the highway recently?

By the grace of God, nothing severe or permanent. Mostly a few blisters, cuts, scraps, bruises, punctures, sprains, minor burns.

In 2012 on BENCHMARK's Leadership Development Retreat, I broke a rib when I didn't jump high enough over a small cord during a problem-solving activity. I landed on my rib cage, but my own hand was under me creating enough pressure for a fracture with the sudden stop of the ground. On a whitewater rafting trip rest stop on a different event, I was standing on the tubes of two rafts when they separated. Doing the splits, I strained a groin muscle.

Hiking out from Chestnut Knob Shelter in Virginia the last day of a Chuck Wilson Memorial Backpack for BENCHMARK was a rough day in 2001. I wasn't feeling well but I had to hike fifteen miles to the van. The group took care of me. I'd hike until they took a break then I would pull out my sleeping bag to sleep while they ate. When they were ready to continue the hike, they'd wake me up, I'd drink some water and they'd hand me some food. I ate while I walked.

Leading trips in the 1990s with the High Road program, there are three instances that come to mind. During transportation from the Upper Peninsula (UP) down to Wisconsin, the canoe trailer attached to the van I was in blew a tire. The driver did an amazing job of keeping us out of on-coming traffic as the van swerved across the white line. In just a few moments we were getting out

AT THIS POINT

of the van that rolled to the passenger side. Half of my student group went to the hospital to get checked out. A few days later I went to an orthopedic to be diagnosed with cervical strain.

I remember backpacking during a storm on an August trip in the UP. We were wading in ankle deep water in a flat swamp during a storm that had more lightening than I preferred. Certainly, much more than the students preferred. Sometimes you just have to keep walking to get out of where you are.

Boundary Waters Canoe Area Wilderness, July 4th, 1999 – The Storm of the Century. Go look it up. The day went from sunny and too warm, to a yellow-green sky very quickly. While we were portaging east out of West Pike Lake, a derecho blew through. We could hear trees falling and snapping. I watched a small duck swim in a portage landing seemingly unfazed by the wind and rain. If the duck wasn't concerned, I didn't think I needed to be either. Standing under a canoe we lodged in a tree for some protection, I prayed, "Lord, if You don't protect us, no one else will." It slowed down our trip considerably since we had to portage canoes over and under the tangle of trees leftover. The storm left its mark for miles and damaged 385,000 acres.

There is significant perceived risk with the activities we utilize on retreats; climbing and rappelling, whitewater rafting and sea kayaking. There is a difference between perceived risk and actual risk. Actual risk is mitigated with preparation, skills training, and incremental learning.

How can I serve?
- Donate the time and treasure, minutes and money.
- collecting interviews from participants
- writing a Soldier or Soldier's child a handwritten note

AT THIS POINT

- serving on a one-day or multi-day ministry event
- pack/unpack, clean and store gear
- videography/photography
- join our bi-monthly prayer team
- lead BENCHMARK's prayer team and take it to greater involvement
- serve as a task force to plan BENCHMARK's 30th anniversary celebration for 2023
- become a member of the BENCHMARK Board of Director to strategically lead this nonprofit ministry

Think of your lowest moment of ministry. What specifically brought you out of that low spot? – C. Landham

Life and ministry are intricately connected. The truth brought me out of it. I began to focus on what is true about God, and about me.

It is difficult to overstate the value of encouragement. When someone whose voice you can trust says, "I see who you are and what God is doing in you; you should keep doing what you're doing, and I'll join you." Sometimes someone else sees what God is doing in you more clearly than you see it yourself. Other times, there is steady confidence that you're on the right path.

These things also help:
- Sleep.
- Journaling.
- My wife.
- My best friend.
- Another dear friend.
- Professional help.
- A loving God who asks me to trust Him.

AT THIS POINT

- A desire to be a faithful man to use all of who I am to honor Christ; temperament, developed skills, inclinations, hurt, and celebration. A small group of people who stepped toward me when I asked.

As you reflect over the years working with young men, has anything had to change in how you communicate and connect?

I've moved to silliness with a dose of sarcasm.

The people we serve often come from a demanding work environment. As quickly as I can I begin to work on some relational connection.

I continue to practice looking people in the eye when I'm talking with someone as much as the setting will allow. I'm asking questions and really listening to the answer that I'm given. A desire to speak the truth in love. I'm known for speaking the "truth," at times brutally. It's still a work in progress to allow the love of Christ to work itself out through me.

I've moved to a clearer introduction to give people an idea of who I am and what BENCHMARK is. It's not enough to say I'm James and I'm with BENCHMARK like my name and the organization's name means anything to them. People need context. So I provide a context from which everything they hear from me will flow. Silly is one of those S's. The other two are serious and sarcastic. I'm in their world not to hurt them but I am there to challenge the way they think. A bit of silliness is helpful.

Can you share one of the most meaningful or memorable experiences of your ministry? – M. Wanca
What is one of the most memorable/meaningful soldier encounters?

AT THIS POINT

We were serving Soldiers from the U.S. Army John F. Kennedy Special Warfare Center and School on a ski/snowboarding ministry event in North Carolina. Soldiers ranged from very young, bus drivers to Special Forces Sergeants who were trainers in that school. During the second evening I was talking about reflection and some of what I've learned from my past. I began to talk about biblical grace and simplifying it to "getting what you do not deserve." After the session, one of the Sergeants was still considering the ideas. So I asked him what he was thinking about. His Catholic background made it difficult for him to understand grace. Perhaps my faith tradition does too. We chatted as a small group of four or five gathered and we were joined by their Chaplain who has a PhD. in theology. What ensued was a forty-five-minute relaxed conversation about the beauty of the grace of God and its meaning in our lives.

We continue to serve, teach, and anticipate other spiritually rich and life-related conversations.

What inspired you to start BENCHMARK? – E. Hodges
Where did the idea to start BENCHMARK come from? – A. Dunlap

BENCHMARK developed from service and ministry I was already involved in; teaching Sunday School/leading workshops/seminars, leading retreats for teenagers and young adults, and instructing wilderness trips, also leading a committee in the local church I attended.

Founding ideas came from my childhood, collegiate and graduate formal education, non-formal education, a college level systematic theology I audited after I finished graduate school,

AT THIS POINT

Bible study, and the significance of a simple benchmark symbol learned while doing land navigation with a map and compass.

I wanted the organization to come alongside local churches so that they could expand their own ministry into adventure for the purpose of leadership development and spiritual growth.

I was working with other people and nonprofits to gain experience and see where my skill and interest could fit.

What has been your greatest challenge leading BENCHMARK? – A. Hicks

People are the greatest challenge. It's either me or someone else. People are also the greatest joy.

It starts with me. My tendency is to procrastinate, to be willful, selfish and undisciplined. I'm reminded of this idea attributed to Socrates, "Let he who would move the world, first move himself." So I keep moving myself. I want to live out these characteristics; truth, love, and wisdom. I also need to live them out in relation to me.

I started BENCHMARK with a supportive wife, some encouragement from others and very little knowledge of how to start/lead a nonprofit ministry. So, I learned from others who were way ahead or a few steps ahead of me. I'm still learning.

I need daily wisdom to better understand on what I need to focus my attention. What do I need to be doing? What do I not need to be doing? Now get to work.

How did you know when to go into full-time ministry with BENCHMARK?

In college the idea of my involvement in full-time ministry was fostered. My first ministry job right out of college required I raised

AT THIS POINT

money like a missionary to be a part of a residential camp and retreat center in eastern Kentucky.

I first and foremost wanted to be a faithful man, faithful to God. I desired to pass on what I had learned and what I was learning to other faithful people who would be able to teach others also.

For about half of the 30 years of BENCHMARK I have been bi-vocational, about half full-time. Stepping toward full-time became the next logical step of faith. I'm still not sure whether I step toward it and God provides, or if God provides and I step toward it. Maybe it's both.

Overall, I've had peace during whatever season I'm in, a clear sense that the Lord was leading me. But there have been seasons, some seasons much longer than I wish, when I wasn't sure I was doing what the Lord wanted me to do. For much of my adult life I have been contentedly discontent and discontentedly content.

How has resilience been a part of your thought processes lately, as the founder of BENCHMARK? – B. Landham

Resilience is the ability to take a hit, learn from it, adjust, and then get back at it. It's developing, over time, mental, emotional, spiritual, and physical depth and drawing from that depth to weather the storms of life to continue on the priorities.

Sometimes the days are long and the nights short. I just have to keep going. What's the next hard thing that needs to be done? It may not be a "fun thing." Go do that now.

It's remembering what I've learned in the past, that I need to do what I can do to get the work done and wait for the Lord to bring help. And He does. Asking for help, helps. But I also have to have a willingness to do what needs to be done, whatever that is, until help arrives.

AT THIS POINT

August 19, 2022
These Colors Have Meaning: Red, Black, White

> *The Christian idea has not been tried and found waiting. It has been found difficult and left untried.* ——G. K. Chesterton

Isn't the world a more interesting place because of color?

We all begin learning our colors when we're young. It's interesting how some colors get ingrained into our minds.

My daddy taught me to hunt. I was a "great" hunter . . . if time on task makes you great at anything. If it was legal to hunt in south Georgia, I likely did. However, I harvested my first and only deer in my fifties, in Tennessee. None before and none since. I hear I had, still have, difficulty sitting still. That's another story.

Did you know that deer see color in muted hues? Blaze orange looks more grayish brownish.[1] Not sure how people learned that piece of information. Because deer have such sharp vision, clothing colors that blend with their environment will help the hunter blend in too. More recent research points to blue, like blue jeans, as a color deer can see very well.[2] Go figure.

Deer just don't see the world in the colors that humans do.

I chuckle when I go to a paint store and look at the wildly erratic color names. Earlier this year we had our stairway wall painted Robust Orange. We could have chosen Ravishing Coral, Emotional, or Invigorate. Yep, those really are color names. And nope, I don't think these colors have meaning. I think it's

AT THIS POINT

marketing, just an attempt to elicit an emotional connection to the color of my walls. Robust Orange is pretty bright.

It's also my daddy who taught me that most fishing lures are made to catch fishermen, first. Perhaps names and colors help with that too.

I grew up in the state of the Georgia Bulldogs. Back in that day, college football, UGA football, was more important than professional sports to many of my friends. Both the Atlanta Braves and the Atlanta Falcons had horrible teams in the 1970s, though the Braves had legendary players like Hank Aaron and Phil Niekro. I wasn't that interested in major league sports. I was more interested in my small-town Little League baseball and my parents were more interested in an acre sized garden in our backyard.

The Falcon's leadership was savvy enough to abscond the basic color palette of the more renowned University of Georgia Bulldogs. Smart move on their part. They apparently knew they needed to make a connection to the college that played "between the hedges." Simple colors; Bulldog Red, Arch Black, and Chapel Bell White.[3] Sounds like UGA named their own colors too.

During the summer the church I attended planned Vacation Bible School (VBS). It was a program for kids from the town to be invited to church for a week of Bible stories, snacks, and crafts. There was a program that parents could come to later. I think ours lasted all morning, but I also recall a night version. It was a big deal in a small town.

It was VBS, or from the local church volunteers, who put on VBS, where I first learned of the Wordless Book.

The Wordless Book is a Christian evangelistic book. Evidence points to it being invented by the famous London Baptist

AT THIS POINT

preacher Charles Haddon Spurgeon, in a message given on January 11, 1866, to several hundred orphans regarding Psalm 51:7 "Wash me, and I shall be whiter than snow." It is called a "book," as it is usually represented with pages.

The preacher Spurgeon's concept contained only three colors:

- black: representing the sinful state of humanity by nature. Usually referred to as the dark page.
- red: representing the blood of Jesus.
- white: representing the perfect righteousness that God has given to believers through the atoning sacrifice of Jesus Christ his Son, usually referred to as the clean page.[4]

We made them out of construction paper, simple books starting with black, red, and white pages then a green page for growth. We must not have had much gold paper in my hometown to represent heaven so a yellow page was added. I've seen the Wordless Book using beads too. It's simple and accurate, just like the gospel of Jesus Christ.

When BENCHMARK needed organizational colors I gravitated toward red, black and white. Wordless Book influenced? Georgia football swayed? Likely both. They are bold, contrasting, straightforward colors. One is a primary color.

I was told by someone who knows organizational promotion far better than I that I should use the color red cautiously. Too much red may not be a good thing. It was a marketing thing.

For years BENCHMARK provided a Bible study bandana to hikers on our Appalachian Trail Outreach in March. Bandanas are

AT THIS POINT

useful on the trail. We also made available water-proof, tear resistant portions of the Bible which were offered at no charge to hikers. Neither of these products are available any longer.

On July 16, 2019, I invited thirty-two people to offer input to design BENCHMARK's first bandana to give to Appalachian Trail hikers in March, especially presented to those who are thru-hiking the entire trail. For five years I'd been wanting BENCHMARK to produce a bandana for our Appalachian Trail Outreach. I had a collection of ideas but it needed focus. Initially I thought of a green bandana with a contrasting color. The hope was for a uniquely BENCHMARK, God honoring, Jesus Christ presenting, outdoor connected, encouraging gift.

A couple of weeks later, I met up with Jeff Coners, an Appalachian Trail thru-hiker, who we served in Georgia in March 2019. A little over four months later, he was in the White Mountains of New Hampshire with over 1800 miles on his legs and far stronger than I. His friend, Nick Isder, was hiking a longer section with him. Jeff was very gracious to let me backpack almost forty miles with them in four days from Zealand Falls Hut to Carter Notch Hut.

Jeff, Nick and I talked about the red bandana project.[6] He had very practical ideas since he's also a follower of Jesus and had spent months with other thru-hikers. Choosing polyester over cotton was a quick decision based on a bandana he had carried since North Carolina. It dries more quickly and doesn't retain odors. His favorite chapter in the Bible is Psalm 31 and it became the center image and content for the whole project.

By taking side trails to get on and off the AT, my five-day total was forty-eight miles. It ranks very high on the list of rugged, beautiful hikes I've done. The bandana guidance I gained was

AT THIS POINT

pivotal. That trip was personally valuable to me for many reasons. I'm thankful for the collaboration with a grad school housemate Stephen Marcy[5] and my best friend Kinley Winchester for both expanding the biblical depth and tightening these ideas for the small space on a bandana. Long-time BENCHMARK staff member Bobby Lawrence recalled staff training for several years incorporating red, black, and white symbolism of the blood of Christ, sin, and purity when we've used a traditional cowboy bandana. His input changed the color scheme. Katie Shull brought the ideas to life with her graphics design. The input from BENCHMARK's Communications Specialist, Chelsea Sánchez, was indispensable. BENCHMARK's bandana became black and white text and images on a very bright red polyester bandana. Every idea doesn't have to die in a committee.

Those of you who know the Wordless Book may be struggling with my order of these colors, red, black, white. Others of you have no idea what I'm talking about. Black, red, white (Wordless Book) to red, black, white because the base color of the bandana is red, reminding me of how much "red" is needed to cover my sinfulness.[6]

Red – Creation shows the greatness of God and His mighty power. (Romans 1:20) God loves you and wants you to know Him personally. He sent Jesus Christ to earth, who lived, died on a cross, and rose from the dead to free you from the penalty of your sin.

"For God so loved the world, that he gave his only Son, that whoever believes in him should not perish but have eternal life" (John 3:16 ESV). He did this so that you can have peace with God and peace in life. (Romans 15:13) "God takes care of all who stay close to him" (Psalm 31 MSG). There's a lot of red on this bandana.

AT THIS POINT

Black – Our sin separates us from God (Romans 5:12,15). The wrong you do, in thought, word, or deed, affects all your decisions and your relationship with God (Romans 8:5-8). Your selfishness inhibits authentic and honest relationships with God and others. "You are in deep, deep trouble" (Psalm 31 MSG).

White – You can turn from your selfishness and the wrong you do to others when you confess your sin to God" (Romans 10:9-10 ESV). Because Jesus Christ conquered sin and death, you can accept the payment He made for your sin to become a new creation, clean, in His sight, reconciled to God (1 John 1:8,9). "Therefore, if anyone is in Christ, he is a new creation. The old has passed away; behold, the new has come" (2 Corinthians 5:17 ESV). "Put your trust in God. He won't let you down" (Psalm 31:9 MSG).

"[I]f you confess with your mouth that Jesus is Lord and believe in your heart that God raised him from the dead, you will be saved. For with the heart one believes and is justified, and with the mouth one confesses and is saved" (Romans 10:9-10 ESV).

What still moves me is that the God of the universe, who created all that exists, knows everything about me, and yet, loves me still. Making a decision to confess your sin and follow Christ is a very personal one.

Just like creating a bandana, doing it in community, connected with others who have similar values, is the way to go. It's far better than living life disconnected.

Red, black, and white remind me of that truth. These colors have meaning.

AT THIS POINT

January 21, 2022
The End: Tell Me "Bye"

> *If you don't know where you're going, you'll probably end up somewhere else.*
> – David Campbell
>
> *Just as people are destined to die once . . .*
> Hebrews 9:27
>
> *If you live long enough, you die.* – James H. Evans

My young wife and I were married only a few months when I landed two jobs on the same day: full-time at A & H Oil and the other delivering Domino's pizza right after the first job.

A & H Oil was started by a former route salesman named Roy T. Alexander. His single-owner Nashville business provided automotive fluids and supplies to mechanics, and mom and pop shops in Middle Tennessee. If it was a fluid that went into a car or truck, we likely sold it. He had his own warehouse built and stocked it with his own money. He'd buy name-brand products by the truckload.

He was frugal, business savvy and country smart. He owned a house up on a hill in Hermitage, Tennessee, and a modest farm in Chapel Hill, Tennessee. Roy T. was a no-nonsense, gruff, swearing, chain-smoker. He was rightfully proud of what he had accomplished.

AT THIS POINT

I was hired to make deliveries.

Every weekday morning at 8:00 sharp we'd have a brief meeting then load two one-ton pickup trucks with the product that was sold the day before, hitting the road to deliver cases of oil, anti-freeze, even the periodic fifty-five-gallon drum.

Though I'd lived in Middle Tennessee during college, I didn't know much about the rural area around Nashville. Roy T., for all practical purposes, had a map of Middle Tennessee in his head, road by road, turn by turn, stop by stop, business by business, owner by owner. I enjoyed learning about Tennessee roads.

I learned to stack case goods on a two-wheeler two wide and six cases high, drive a tow motor, stack product pallets three high, and clean up spilled oil. We clocked out at 5:00 p.m.

My very first day of work, Roy T. barked orders, literal orders, to pack on the truck in reverse. The last stop was packed first. He knew how to pyramid stack boxes every which way to maximize truck capacity. It was a simple, efficient system.

Before cell phones, Google, Waze, or Apple maps, Roy T. gave me detailed directions of every stop, turn by turn. I took feverish notes.

Standing on the dock looking at the loaded truck, he handed me the invoices for the day and said, "Tell me bye."

I looked at him puzzled.

He said again, "Tell me bye!"

I said, "Bye?"

With that he turned on his heels and went back to his office leaving me standing on the dock by myself.

I figured it out. I got in the truck and left.

In time he grew to trust me.

AT THIS POINT

I came back to the warehouse one afternoon and he yelled for me to come to the office. That's normally not a good thing. He asked me about a particular stop and what happened. I told him as well as I could. Roy T. said the customer called to complain about something I did and the customer told him that I had cussed him. And with little hesitation Roy T. told the business that I had not cussed him and that they'd not be doing business anymore. We never stopped at that business again.

Later I became a route salesman, which I wasn't very good at, and then when a long-time employee passed away, I was asked to process accounts receivable and walkup sales. With adjoining offices, he let me install a small exhaust fan between my office and his to vent cigarette smoke.

He'd answer the phone, "A & H Oil." With a bit of silence, I'd hear, "Are you buying or selling?" Then I'd hear again, "Are you buying or selling?"

Slamming the phone down meant someone was trying to avoid giving him a straight answer and he was done. It was his business and he could do what he wanted.

The day before Thanksgiving we were all called into the office and given a "bonus," cash, just like a former boss of his had done. Every year, he told us that he gave us cash, so that, if for no other reason, we'd have something to be thankful for on Thanksgiving.

Roy T. took his best friend, another employee, and me to my one and only NASCAR race at Talladega. It was something! Fast cars, loud noise, and people standing on the backs of their seats so that often I was only looking at someone else's seat.

He knew I had other possibilities on my mind. For a semester he allowed me to come in "late" a couple of days a week so I

AT THIS POINT

could teach an 8 a.m. college class at a Bible College. I'd change from a shirt and tie to my work clothes. He never deducted my pay. When I left during the summer of 1990 to train as a wilderness instructor, he hired me back when I returned.

He told me that if he had a son, he'd want him to be like me.

Some years after I left the company, I attended Roy T.'s funeral in about 2001 with "tell me 'bye'" still ringing in my ears.

The day will come when I no longer roam this planet. It's a sure reality, for all of us, unless Jesus comes back first. I have some thoughts about the end.

"And someday sooner than you think you'll see me face to face" is a phrase that gives me pause and makes me smile all at the same time. It's from the song The Promise.[1]

I've been to a few funerals. Not nearly as many as some of my friends. I can't imagine what it's like to be a pastor or military Chaplain or funeral director. One day this body will be at my funeral. I'll be somewhere else. There is a finality to a funeral. I hope to have one.

My funeral should be joyful. Maybe a little serious, a little silly, and perhaps a bit sarcastic. A fitting end.

I hope for laughter and smiling about a life well lived. That I'll be remembered as someone who did more than I thought I would. That people showed me more grace than I ever deserved. That I was funny at times and just laughable at other times. That I grew to be a more content and joyful person. That my quirky sense of humor was more of an asset rather than a liability.

I will be joyful. I'm not here. I've gone to the relationship I have valued most. I've gone ahead and will wait for you to join

AT THIS POINT

me with Christ in heaven because my faith is in Christ, not in what I've done.

More than one teacher, preacher or writer has posed the question: "What do you want to be said of you at your funeral?" I've looked ahead at what I would like to be true of me.

Maybe they'll have kind things to say. Maybe their lives are better because I existed, especially my family. I hope they sincerely realize that I grew in my love for them. That I matured to manage my emotions and actions better than when they were younger. That I loved them and I would do–and did do–anything I was capable of doing which was in their best interest.

My tombstone would have whatever important information needs to be there. I was born and then I died. It could read: HARD-HEADED, IMPERFECT, FOLLOWER OF JESUS CHRIST

Oh, wait, no tombstone for me. I really want my ashes strewn on the Appalachian Trail (AT) at Gooch Gap near Suches, Georgia. This is the place where I have spent more time than any other place on the AT with so many other people. I've served there. Cooked food. Sat by campfires. Weighed and shook out backpacks for hikers. Prayed there. Laughed there. Cried there. It's a fitting location for my dust to go back to dust.

At my funeral, there should be singing. I like to sing. I grew up in the First Free Will Baptist Church of Jesup, Georgia, and we sang hymns every time we met together. I grew to love many hymns because many of them were really stabilizing. When I was a kid there weren't that many praise and worship songs, though I have grown in my appreciation of the beauty and richness of those too.

As a teenager cleaning the church with my dad and brother, I have very clear memories of singing a Fanny Crosby song in the

AT THIS POINT

far back short rows of that sanctuary, muffled by the roar of a vacuum. I cried singing this song pleading with God for His guidance. Singing it because I wanted it to be true. Growing up as a teenager is hard, even in the best of circumstances. Even as an adolescent I saw in this song what I wanted to be my present and my future. And since then, I've sung these words on many miles of trail, still occasionally tearing up. These lyrics still stick with me today and I want them to be my declaration.

All The Way My Savior Leads Me[2]
    All the way my Savior leads me–
    What have I to ask beside?
    Can I doubt His tender mercy,
    Who through life has been my guide?
    Heav'nly peace, divinest comfort,
    Here by faith in Him to dwell!
    For I know, whate'er befall me,
    Jesus doeth all things well;
    For I know, whate'er befall me,
    Jesus doeth all things well.

    All the way my Savior leads me–
    Cheers each winding path I tread,
    Gives me grace for ev'ry trial,
    Feeds me with the living bread.
    Though my weary steps may falter
    And my soul athirst may be,
    Gushing from the rock before me,
    Lo! a spring of joy I see;

AT THIS POINT

Gushing from the rock before me,
Lo! A spring of joy I see.

All the way my Savior leads me—
Oh, the fullness of His love!
Perfect rest to me is promised
In my Father's house above.
When my spirit, clothed immortal,
Wings its flight to realms of day,
This my song through endless ages:
Jesus led me all the way;
This my song through endless ages:
Jesus led me all the way.

Fanny Crosby, 1875

Though I'm not a public singer of songs, the 1993 song by Geoff Moore and the Distance, When All Is Said And Done, also sums my thoughts up well. I still listen to it periodically.

When All Is Said And Done[3]

When the music fades into the past,
When the days of life are through,
What will be remembered of where I've come?
When all is said and done?

Will they say I loved my family?
That I was a faithful friend?

AT THIS POINT

That I lived to tell of God's own son?
When all is said and done.

Of how I longed to see the hour,
When I would hear that trumpet sound.
So I could rise and see my Savior's face,
And see him smile,
And say "Well done."

You can forget my name
And the songs I've sung,
Every line and every tune.
But remember the truth of Jesus' love,
When all is said and done
When all is said and done.

    At this point, there it is. The end. The end of the journey of a hard-headed, imperfect follower of Jesus Christ. "Be very careful, then, how you live—not as unwise but as wise, making the most of every opportunity, because the days are evil" (Ephesians 5:15,16).
    I encourage you "to remember the truth of Jesus' love, when all is said and done."[3]
    Tell me "bye."

AT THIS POINT

ENDNOTES

Preface
[1] Philip Yancey, Soul Survivor: How my Faith Survived the Church. (New York: Random House/ Doubleday Religion, 2001), 253. Excerpt(s) from SOUL SURVIVOR: HOW MY FAITH SURVIVED THE CHURCH by Philip Yancey, copyright© 2001 by Someone Cares Charitable Trust. Used by permission of Doubleday, an imprint of the Knopf Doubleday Publishing Group, a division of Penguin Random House LLC. All rights reserved.

BENCHMARK's R3 Toward Resilience
Part 1

Introduction
[1] Oxford English Dictionary, 2nd ed. (Oxford: Oxford University Press, 2004), s.v. "zeitgeist."
[2] Master Resilience Training (MRT)
https://www.benning.army.mil/MCoE/R2/R2-Master.html
[3] Chaplain's Creed

Chapter 1
[1] Tommy Yessick, Building Blocks for Longer Life and Ministry. (Nashville: Convention Press, 1997), 105-112.

Chapter 2
[1] Thurman, Chris. The Lies We Believe. Nashville: Thomas Nelson Publishers, 1989.

AT THIS POINT

[2]https://www.army.mil/values/
[3]Warren W. Wiersbe. Be Rich. (Colorado Springs: David C. Cook, 1979), 107. Excerpted from Be Rich © 1979 by Warren W. Wiersbe. Used by permission of David C Cook. May not be further reproduced. All rights reserved.
[4]Stephen Covey. The 7 Habits of Highly Effective People: Powerful Lessons in Personal Change. (New York: Simon & Schuster, 1989), 71.

Chapter 4
[1]Charles Swindoll. Come Before Winter. (Portland: Multnomah Press, 1985), 23.
[2]https://www.benning.army.mil/Infantry/ARTB/Student-Information
[3]https://www.outsideonline.com/2411895/army-ranger-school#close
[4]https://www.wearethemighty.com/articles/this-is-everything-you-need-to-know-about-army-rangers
[5]Twitter post, December 7, 2020
https://twitter.com/maxgilliam11/status/1336018488524042240/photo/1

Hit by a Truck
[1]Wayne Memorial Hospital, Discharge Summary, J.W. Brantley, MD. Physical Finding
Revealed multiple abrasions, contusions throughout with the severest injury being the right knee, where he had complete avulsion of the skin overlying the kneecap with exposure of the patella & partial tear of the patella ligament. There was a severe contusion also at the right angle with x-ray evidence of a fracture of the fibula & some separation of the medial epiphysis of the malleolus. February 25, 1974

Chapter 5
[1]Dallas Willard. The Great Omission. (San Francisco: HarperOne, 2014), 61.

AT THIS POINT

[2] Albert Barnes. Barnes Notes: Ephesians to Philemon. (Grand Rapids: Baker Book House, 1983), 205. (public domain)
[3] F. Leroy Forlines. Systematic Theology. (Nashville: Randall House Publications, 1975), 47.
[4] Sam Allberry. James for You. (South-West London, UK: The Goodbook Company, 2015).
[5] Warren W. Wiersbe. Be Mature. (Wheaton: Victor Books, 1981), 112.

Chapter 6
[1] Oxford English Dictionary, 2nd ed. (Oxford: Oxford University Press, 2004), s.v. "Pollyanna."

Chapter 7
[1] Andy Stanley. "Ask It." Your Move (podcast). January – February 2014. Accessed July 2016. The description of Part 1: "Question Everything" states: "What if there was a question that would clarify your best option for ninety percent of the decisions you make in life—a question that answers just about everything? It would have the potential to foolproof your relationships, marriage, finances, calendar, pace, and health. It would reduce the complexity of your life. It would save you time, money, and tears. You would carry around less regret. And best of all, you wouldn't have to apologize nearly as much.

Of every invitation, opportunity, relationship, or decision, ask, "What's the wise thing to do?" If you were going to do the wise thing, what would it be? By asking that question, even if you don't follow through, you will discover something about you.

You owe it to yourself to know the answer to that question."
[2] The Mountaineers. Mountaineering: Freedom of the Hills, 9th Edition. (Seattle: The Mountaineers Books) 2017.

Chapter 8
[1] George MacDonald. The Wise Woman. Grand Rapids: Wm. B. Eerdmans Publishing Co, 1980), 23.

AT THIS POINT

Mama and Daddy
[1]Michael Card. "Sunrise of Your Smile," track 13 on Scribbling in the Sand, Covenant Artists, LLC., compact disc. Copyright © 1994 Birdwing Music (ASCAP) PHIL NAISH (ASCAP) (adm. at CapitolCMGPublishing.com) All rights reserved. Used by permission.
[2]Family history added by my brother, John B. (Joby) Evans, Jr.

Reflection toward a Resilient Life
Part 2

What Soup Do You Swim In?: A Taste of Today's Culture
[1]This article previously published by Randall House Publications, April 10, 2009.

I Still Remember
[1]Gary Driskell. "Another Time, Another Place," track 2 on Another Time...Another Place, Word Records, 1990, compact disc. Words and Music by Gary Driskell © 1990 Curb Word Music (ASCAP) and Housewife Music (ASCAP). All rights administered by WC Music Corp.

Yet Another Blog
[1]http://www.despair.com/blogging.html

Happy Easter. He's Alive.
[1]James Bryan Smith. Embracing the Love of God: The Path & Promise of Christian Life. New York: HarperCollins Publishers, 1995), 83.

Fast & reFocus
[1]Richard J. Foster. Celebration of Discipline. (New York: Harper & Row, Publishers, 1978), 48.

AT THIS POINT

Fifteen Minutes Matter
[1]Stephen R. Covey. The 7 Habits of Highly Effective People: Powerful Lessons in Personal Change. (New York: Simon & Schuster, 1989), 161.

4x4x48: Toward Birthday Endurance
[1]Michael Card. "Sunrise of Your Smile," track 13 on Scribbling in the Sand, Covenant Artists, LLC., compact disc. Copyright © 1994 Birdwing Music (ASCAP) PHIL NAISH (ASCAP) (adm. at CapitolCMGPublishing.com) All rights reserved. Used by permission.

[2]"Annually the United States Army Ranger Training Brigade sponsors the arduous Best Ranger Competition at Fort Benning, Georgia. Now known as the "Lt. Gen. David E. Grange Jr. Best Ranger Competition," the event began in May 1982 as a contest among members of the various training camps of the Ranger Training Brigade (then the Ranger Department). From that modest beginning it has expanded to include teams from Special Operations, Army Ranger, and airborne-qualified units. In addition, teams representing other services, foreign forces, and the Army National Guard enter the fray to prove their mettle. While some competitors arrive just wanting "to finish," most are determined "to win." During the competition, two-man buddy teams go head-to-head, Ranger style, overcoming 62 near continuous hours of physically, emotionally, and intellectually demanding challenges to earn the title of the "best" 2-person Ranger buddy team. In the words of LTG (Ret.) David Grange, "This competition is not just to see who is the toughest or the most physically fit. It is to see who is mentally the strongest, the most determined to finish." https://www.ausa.org/tips-preparing-best-ranger-competition

Be Still or Act
[1]Reuben Morgan. "Still," track 6 on Hope, Hillsong Music Publishing, 2002. Compact disc.

AT THIS POINT

Copyright © 2002 Hillsong Music Publishing (APRA) (adm. in the US and Canada at CapitolCMGPublishing.com) All rights reserved. Used by permission.

BENCHMARK History/Foundations
Part 3

We're OK
[1]https://www.military.com/daily-news/2020/04/18/military-travel-ban-extended-until-june-30-some-restrictions-eased.html

These Colors Have Meaning
[1]https://www.nhcf.org/what-were-up-to/what-colors-can-deer-see/
[2]https://deerassociation.com/can-deer-see-blaze-orange/
[3]https://teamcolorcodes.com/georgia-bulldogs-color-codes/
[4]Wordless Book https://en.wikipedia.org/wiki/Wordless_Book
[5]Read more from Stephen Marcy at The Truth of the Gospel, https://goodnewsapologetics.com
[6]https://benchmark.org/bandana/

Ask the Founder, almost anything, about BENCHMARK Adventure Ministries
[1]https://en.wikipedia.org/wiki/Women_in_the_United_States_Army

The End: Tell Me "Bye"
[1]Brian Gene White/Don Poythress. "The Promise," track 3 on Above It All, Spring Hill Music Group, 2003, compact disc. Copyright © 2002 Universal Music - Brentwood Benson Tunes (SESAC) (adm. at CapitolCMGPublishing.com) All rights reserved. Used by permission.
[2]Fanny Crosby. "All The Way My Savior Leads Me," 1875. https://hymnary.org/text/all_the_way_my_savior_leads_me

AT THIS POINT

[3]Geoff Moore/Jeff Silvey. "When All Is Said And Done," track 10 on Evolution, 1993, compact disc. Copyright © 1993 Birdwing Music (ASCAP) Songs On The Forefront (SESAC) (adm. at CapitolCMGPublishing.com) All rights reserved. Used by permission.

AT THIS POINT

Influential Books
(*– top 10)

Barton, Ruth Haley. Strengthening the Soul of Your Leadership: Seeking God in the Crucible of Ministry. Downers Grove, IL: InterVarsity Press, 2015. (Unabridged Audiobook)

Borthwick. Paul. Feeding Your Forgotten Soul. Grand Rapids: Zondervan, 1990.

Brown, Brené. The Gifts of Imperfection. Center City: Hazelden, 2021.

Chambers, Oswald. My Utmost for His Highest: An Updated Edition in Today's Language. Grand Rapids: Discovery House Publishers, 1992.

Collins, Jim. Good to Great: Why Some Companies Make the Leap and Others Don't. New York: HarperBusiness, 2001.

*Corbett, Steve and Brian Fikkert. When Helping Hurts: How to Alleviate Poverty Without Hurting the Poor . . . and Yourself. Chicago: Moody Publishers, 2009.

*Covey, Stephen. The Seven Habits of Highly Effective People. New York: Simon & Schuster, 1989.

Durant, Michael J. and Steven Hartov. The Night Stalkers. New York: Penguin Group, 2006.

Eldridge, John. Wild at Heart: Discovering the Secret of a Man's Soul. Nashville: Nelson Books/Thomas Nelson Publishers, 2001.

AT THIS POINT

Farrar, Steve. Finishing Strong. Sisters, OR: Multnomah Books, 1995.

*Foster, Richard J. Celebration of Discipline. New York: Harper & Row, Publishers, 1978.

*Frankl, Viktor E. Man's Search for Meaning. New York: Washington Square Press, 1959.

Gladwell, Malcolm. Outliers: The Story of Success. Hachette Audio, 2008. (Unabridged Audiobook)

*Grant, J. Howard. Balancing Life's Demands: A New Perspective on Priorities. Portland: Multnomah Press, 1983.

Greer, Peter. The Spiritual Danger of Doing Good. Minneapolis, MN: Bethany House/Baker Publishing House, 2013.

Herold, Cameron. Double Double: How to Double Your Revenue and Profit in 3 Years or Less. Greenleaf Book Group, 2011. (Unabridged Audiobook)

Hollingsworth, Amy. The Simple Faith of Mr. Rogers. Nashville: Thomas Nelson Publishing, 2012.

*Kalisch, Ken. The Role of the Instructor in the Outward Bound Educational Process. Kearney, NE: Morris, 1979.

Keller, Timothy. The King's Cross: The Story of the World in the Life of Jesus. Penguin Audio, 2011.

*MacDonald, George. The Wise Woman. Grand Rapids: Wm. B. Eerdmans Publishing Co, 1980.

AT THIS POINT

MacDonald, Gordon. Ordering Your Private World. Nashville: Thomas Nelson Publishing, 2003.

Myrer, Anton. Once an Eagle. New York: Harper Perennial Modern Classics/HarperCollins Publishers; Reprint edition, 2013. (Audiobook)

Peters, Thomas J, and Robert H. Waterman, Jr. In Search of Excellence: Lesson from America's Best-Run Companies. New York: Warner Books, 1982.

Peterson, Eugene H. A Long Obedience in the Same Direction. Downers Grove, IL: InterVarsity Press, 1980.

Phillips, J.B. Your God Is Too Small. New York: Collier Books/Macmillan Publishing Company, 1961.

Piper, John. Don't Waste Your Life. Wheaton, IL: Crossway Books/Good News Publishers, 2003.

Shaeffer, Francis. The Mark of a Christian. Downers Grove, IL: InterVarsity Press, 1970.

*Smith, James Bryan. Embracing the Love of God: The Path & Promise of Christian Life. New York: HarperCollins Publishers, 1995.

Swindoll, Charles. The Quest for Character. Portland: Multnomah Press, 1987.

Thurman, Chris. The Lies We Believe. Nashville: Thomas Nelson Publishers, 1989.

von Oech, Roger. A Whack on the Side of the Head: How You Can be More Creative. New York: Warner Books, Inc., 1983.

AT THIS POINT

Whitney, Donald. Spiritual Disciplines for the Christian Life. Colorado Springs: Navpress, 1991.

Wiersbe, Warren. Be Rich. Colorado Springs: David C. Cook, 1979.

Willink, Jocko and Leif Babin. Extreme Ownership: How U.S. Navy SEALs Lead and Win. Macmillan Audio, 2015.

*Yancey, Philip. Soul Survivor: How My Faith Survived the Church. New York: Doubleday/Random House, 2001.

*Yessick, Tommy. Building Blocks for Longer Life and Ministry. Nashville: Convention Press, 1997.

AT THIS POINT

AT THIS POINT

AT THIS POINT

AT THIS POINT

www.ingramcontent.com/pod-product-compliance
Lightning Source LLC
Chambersburg PA
CBHW070649120526
44590CB00013BA/885